I0888885

Nightsun

ISSUE #25

FALL 2006

ALICIA OSTRIKER

GUEST EDITOR

F R O S T B U R G   S T A T E   U N I V E R S I T Y

Nightsun

Issue #25   Fall 2006

GUEST EDITOR: Alicia Ostriker

MANAGING EDITOR: Gerry LaFemina

DESIGN: Colleen Stump

COVER PHOTOGRAPH: *View south. Terrace Street, Manayunk, Philadelphia. 1995* by Martin J. Desht

INTERNS: Joan Fleck and Alan Carey

Nightsun is published annually by the Frostburg State University Center for Creative Writing and appreciates the support of Frostburg State University's College of Liberal Arts and Sciences and Department of English. Additional support from the Allegany Arts Council of Maryland is also appreciated.

Please visit our website: www.frostburg.edu/cwcenter/nightsun.htm for information about submissions and the next issue's guest editor.

Subscriptions: Single issues are $9.00 plus $2.00 postage and handling. A two-issue subscription is $15.00 postage and handling included. Subscription orders and manuscripts should be sent to *Nightsun*, College of Liberal Arts and Sciences, Frostburg State University, 101 Braddock Road, Frostburg, Maryland 21532-2303. Make checks payable to "FSU for *Nightsun*."

FROSTBURG STATE UNIVERSITY

ALLEGANY ARTS COUNCIL

Printed on recycled paper
ISBN 1-878306-17-0
Copyright 2006

CONTENTS

1 EDITOR'S PAGE

2 KIM ADDONIZIO
Bus Stop in Front of the Church of the Most Holy Redeemer
Migrations

4 ANITA BARROWS
Notes in the Aftermath
Black sow

8 ROBIN BECKER
To a Poet

9 DAN BELLM
Book of Numbers

14 KURT BROWN
At the Summer Lake Club

16 CHRIS BURSK
Civil War in Seventh Period

18 HAYDEN CARRUTH
In Memoriam

20 JAN CLAUSEN
Pigs Advance as Organ-Transplant Factories for People

22 CHARD DeNIORD
Enkidu's Lament

23 DENISE DUHAMEL
Win Chinese Buffet

26 STEPHEN DUNN
Returning to the Ravens

27 ANN FISHER-WIRTH
Army Men

30 JEFF FRIEDMAN
Crows
Video Game

32 ROSS GAY
Prayer for My Unborn Niece or Nephew

34 REGINALD GIBBONS
Samaritan

37 ALBERT GOLDBARTH
Drongo

40 JIM HABA
The Window
Listen, Friends

42 MARILYN HACKER
Ghazal: Across the Street

43 DONALD HALL
Gospel

44 ELOISE KLEIN HEALY
Flower Shop

46 LORRAINE HEALY
Where They Were
AP Photo: Two Rwandan Women Reunited in a Church in Kabiza, 1997

50 JANE HIRSHFIELD
Shadow: An Assay

52 ILYA KAMINSKY
We Lived Happily During the War
Brother

54 MARILYN KRYSL
Not in Our Names
Bulldozer Sestina: Rafa, 2004

57 MARTIN DESHT
Warnock Street, Philadelphia. 1998
Mechanic and Hill Streets, Southside Bethlehem, Pa. 1998
North Broad, near Parrish Street, Philadelphia. 1997
York and Clarion Streets, Philadelphia. 1998
"Honest Lou's Pest Control." North Broad Street, Philadelphia. 1997
Rolling Mills and Coke Works. Bethlehem Steel Corp. Bethlehem, Pa. 1990

63 JOAN LARKIN
Inaugural
Rouen, 1431

65 DORIANNE LAUX
The Long Goodbye

67 DAVID LEHMAN
Poem in the Manner of Gullaume Apollinaire

68 ANNE MARIE MACARI
Migration South
Ants

72 PABLO MEDINA
Not All Of Me

73 D.H. MELHEM
Rant Inspired by Frank Rich, "We Do Not Torture" and Other Funny Stories

74 ED OCHESTER
March of the Penguins

75 ROBERT PINSKY
Two Arias from "Death and the Powers"

78 HILDA RAZ
Pantoum
September 11

80 JASON SCHNEIDERMAN
College Application Essay
Theodor Adorno

82 YERRA SUGARMAN
From Journal: Rai'ut Coma Ward, Tel Aviv-Yaffo, July 2003

83 RICHARD TAYSON
On the Way to See James Dean

87 RONALD WALLACE
Inner City

88 IRENE WILLIS
The Wilders

89 ELEANOR WILNER
In a Time of War
Afterwards

93 DAHLIA RAVIKOVITCH
The Story of the Arab Who Died in the Fire

94 RIVKA MIRIAM
These Mountains: Selected Poems of Rivka Miriam

95 BORIS VIAN
The Deserter

97 EMILY MANN
Mrs. Packard (1st Scene)

107 CONTRIBUTORS

Lyric, narrative, meditation, satire, elegy, rant. Sonnet, sestina, tercet, pantoum, blank verse, "free" verse. Memory and imagination. Tenderness, fear, fury, grief, love, despair, desire. Street scenes, road scenes, combat scenes, farm animals, allegorical birds and insects, parody, comedy, prayer. Wars and the aftermath of wars. The twentieth and twenty-first centuries, but also the fifteenth. Biblical tales and Babylonian myths alive today as in the world of our ancestors, for, as Faulkner said in his Nobel speech, "the past is not dead. It is not even past." The world of religion, the world of nature, the world of the barbershop, the mall, the movie house, the airport terminal, the diner, the refugee camp. The world of the self and its shadow. Sexuality and dread and violence.

Poems of subtle refinement, poems of crude anger.

It is what I hoped for. When soliciting work for this issue, I asked to see writing that grappled with history and politics. I had a thirst to satisfy. I wished, in this small way, to demonstrate how deep and various poetry with a public dimension can be, how forcefully it can speak to our spirits, how elegantly or exuberantly it can outlive its occasion.

"Try to praise the mutilated world," says the Polish poet Adam Zagajewski. The writing in this issue of *Nightsun* does so, simply by existing. Some of it made me laugh, some made me cry. Much of it took my breath away. It is an honor to share this writing with you.

~ Alicia Ostriker

Bus Stop in Front of the Church of the Most Holy Redeemer

There is no bus. The sign is here
to mark the place

a bus once was.
The stained cement shows

where someone dragged himself
bleeding after a drive-by.

Beyond the shelter
of scratched plastic, the torn schedule

behind crazed glass,
one shoe's been carefully set

upright in the weeds,
encircled with shards

of busted bottles that catch
the late light and blaze. It's holy

to wait, while cars and lives pass.
To believe there is a bus,

that you can hear it coming
a long way off through the darkening streets.

Migrations

Over the pond, a shabby group
of undershirts was passing,
barely clearing the barbed wire
of the pasture fence. From a blind
on the far side hunters kept firing

and one or two shirts dropped
fluttering into the sedge and pampas.
Then came the panties and nylons,
skimming the water to see their reflections;
they fell torn and bloodied, clogging the water

and men came to fish them out with long hooked poles.
For a while the sky was clear,
but it was the season, and soon the flyway
was crowded again: above the treeline
baseball caps sailed past, scarves, plaid shorts,

and uniforms — a steady stream as far as the eye could see.
Above them the stiff white shirts
were aligned in a precise V. And higher,
where the clouds would be, the elegant suits
traveled, slow and stately,

though occasionally one spread its sleeves
and circled, then plunged straight down
to ravage the flocks below
making a kind of ragged hole
the others flapped harder to fill in.

Notes in the Aftermath (Bosnia/Croatia)

1

A darkness surrounds us, how
will we find our way through it?
We go out to buy milk, bread.
Someone teaches the children a rhyme
about geese, or the sea. We come home,
cook supper, play with the dog.
Meanwhile leaves are falling.
Someone reaches for another's hand, or holds
her face in her own hands.
At the bottom of a ravine, a creek
is singing and singing. Don't you see
how the sky has moved suddenly
closer to the houses? Furiously
we are writing notes to the infinite,
we are saying *this, this, this.*

2

What can I offer except
as witness. I have no faith
that the thread will catch, will catch

again ~ yet look, it catches.

3

I wrap the child Ivana
in a towel, Ivana who has just
taken a swim in the Adriatic.
I hold her shivering flesh
against my flesh,
feel in her eight year old body

the explosion she saw
when she was six –

shards and flame and her mother
lying dead on the street before her.
Schoolbooks, the contents of a purse.

Hot sunlight beats down. Ivana's small, scarred fingers
twist my hair. I keep her warm.

I would hold her
as long as it took
to walk back
to wherever it was

that day should have
led them: the noisy lunchroom,
the playground, the schoolchildren singing.

The lipstick, the folded papers
neatly inside the purse. Ivana
waving goodbye to her mother

at the schoolyard gate.

4

Let me be witness then.

Black sow

Polly, feed now the black sow
(English Renaissance song)

1

Let those who are hungry eat
Let the mist rise from the grass

and the grass be soaked, though there is not yet rain.

Let the grain spill abundantly from the hands
of Polly your servant, who only

once these have been fed
will sit down at the table.

2

The leaves of the quaking aspen are radiant yellow
before the first frost; then
brown, brown as any leaves.

Come, sorrowing one, despised one.
Aren't you lonely out there,
lingering over whatever it is that keeps you?
Though you are muscular I see
where your softness reveals itself

between the coarse black hairs.

3

Come for your supper now. Call
the animals in from the fields.
Who does not come will not eat. A wind
darkens the water of the pond.

Here is the day's slop:
hours spent looking out a window,
a letter not written, a work unfinished.
Someone's hand on a table, absently drumming. Come

from the far place where you have been poking
all morning and afternoon
in cold mud, in stony earth. Come, black sow. Come night,
come sadness. Come birds

lifting into the sky from the tips of the grasses.
Don't you believe

we have something yet to give you?

To A Poet

Because the young men spoke of you with reverence,
raising their voices and glasses all over Cambridge;
because you were drunk and missed the toilet,
expecting a woman to clean up your mess;
because I had spent years reading your work;
because Bishop and Dickinson meant little to you
who championed the working class
but had no patience for angry women—
I could not see the thing we shared, our shared
contempt for bureaucrats and department chairs,
the paperwork and pomposity of the institutions,
the true-believers, the deans in their decorous hoods.
Each morning, far from you, I line my briefcase
with the headlines, bear my tenure across the green.

Book of Numbers

(A war diary)

1. (In the wilderness)

Out in the open, in the midst of life,
Set apart in an unsettled place,
We counted ourselves, and recounted, in unbelief
And dread – we wanted to be numberless
As stars, but we were dust. Another war
Was near, and would we add or measure up?
Calculating constantly, unsure
Of our own strength, gathered troop by troop
Under our flags and banners, sounding the horn,
Trumping up our size with a few zeroes
Here and there, accountable to none,
God's glory on our side, we came to feel like heroes.
But no. Did I say *we?* I kept my pride.
Holier than thou, I stood aside.

Bemidbar, Num. 1:1 – 4:20

2. (Nazirite)

I stood aside; I was holier than thou –
But in the end they numbered all of us.
Which reminds me of a war some time ago:
I had let my hair grow long; I was serious,
Which was half the point. *You won't stop any war, you know,*
By making yourself look like a girl, Dad said –
Is that what you are? If I could have made a vow
And stood apart, I would have, but instead,
I was stuck with the men; I was supposed to fight;
My number was up; I had won the lottery.
Dad turned to go. I raised my voice to a shout
For once – *You come back here and talk to me* –
And saw the fear in his eye. This was not my plan.
But having won, I walked to town, and got my hair cut, like a man.

Naso, Num. 4:21 – 7:89

3. (Smoke)

And having "won" the "war," we'd won the right
To watch the fallen city burn – by night
The very likeness of a fire, by day a cloud
Of poison smoke – and were we satisfied?
The times were bad. Our money was no good.
We whined like riffraff. Then we felt alone.
Why did the nations hate us so? Where would
We ever in this world feel safe again?
Time to get tough: you can call it slavery
But a little less freedom, and we might feel free.
O fleshpots of Egypt! How hungry we were,
Though we choked on what we'd got; how could we trust
There would ever be enough? We had come this far,
And here: this was not the land God promised us.

Beha'alotecha, Num. 8:1 – 12:16

4. (Milk and honey)

O dear God: the land You have promised us
Already has people living in it; and why
Didn't we hear that part before the exodus?
So this is the choice, to live as slaves or die
As slaves to war. Now think: some other place
You haven't got? We sent out men to spy
For us, a sorry lot who claim a race
Of giants lives up there, but what a lie –
Most likely long-lost relatives. Hebron's
A town as old as Esau, walled with stones
They'll gladly throw at us, blood brothers or not.
Couldn't we come in peace, share what we've got
Including You, settle down and call
It off? But *No*, You answer. *You must dispossess them all.*

Shelach-lecha, Num. 13:1 – 15:41

5. (Evidence)

Stand back – while I annihilate them all!
And it was as if the earth had swallowed them
With their fire-pans of mass destruction – hell
If we could find a trace – a thing unknown
In God's creation! Where had the bad guys gone?
The President was *mad*. Now half the damn
Rabble he'd liberated were on his case:
Are you going to kill us, too? You've gone too far.
You have too much. His men went house to house
Looking for trouble, and finding it, but where
Was the evidence he needed to confound
These stiff-necked people? Guess it's gone underground
Ha ha – and if that kind of story satisfies you,
Then let the earth open its mouth and take me, too.

Korach, Num. 16:1 – 18:32

6. (The well)

Could the earth open its mouth if we told it to,
And bring forth water, even from a rock?
The taint of so much death, now what will wash?
We brought them rule by our people, the holy cow
Of freedom, and made a burnt sacrifice: now Iraq
Had no water to drink but what was mixed with ash.
Some drank out of old sludge barrels days on end
With the stray death fire of Sheol barely rinsed off.
We set snakes loose. And the oil flowed again:
Spring up, o well. This generation will die,
And we will not cross over, Adonai,
Because we have not believed in freedom enough.
The land was never ours, and what we do
Is play at sojourners here, who but pass through.

Chukat, Num. 19:1 – 22:1

7. (Cease fire, Jerusalem, June 20)

I am but a sojourner here, and come past due,
Cause of my stubborn ways, on my brazen ass:
Balaam son of Peor, whose eye is true,
Take you up a superior vantage point and curse
This people. How can I curse? *Ma tovu*
Ohalecha Ya'akov: How fair: Only to bless
With the word God puts in my mouth: No siren or blast
In the land, no harm in sight, no woe in view
For Israel: Late light of evening over
The quiet streets, and people stepping from
Their houses to go walking: And to the brother
Enemy you've left without a home,
O nation, peace: For what the spirit tells, I say.
Now I will turn toward home, and go my way.

Balak, Num. 22:2 – 25:9

8. (Illinois, July 4)

Our boy has come home, but the war doesn't go away,
O sons of Peoria, by wishing it so:
An answered prayer: *God bless the USA,*
Where at least I know I'm free, but do we know?
We hardly ask, and our soldier doesn't say
Much, what he's seen or done: We have a ways to go:
There are songs of exultation and zealotry
Downtown at dusk, bombs bursting in air, to show
Us who we are, forever asking God
To unbless someone else. O awful pride
Of nationhood, resentful, paranoid,
A little desperate, as if the one who heard
All prayer were some diligent American God,
Numbering the living and the dead.

Pinchas, Num. 25:10 – 30:1

9. (Uday and Qusay / Wolf and Snake)

Numbering two more among the dead
From off the master vengeance list – *o let*
Me see the scary part, the suffering,
O let me look at the scars – we are rifling
Through the mortified, mortared place – *we have destroyed*
Their line – meaning, no further enemy?
Shock troops at the instance of the Lord,
And fairy-tale demons: the laid-out staring
corpse-faces: and whose vision shall I see
With now, washing the strain away, word
Of God, passing through fire and water what we
Saw and did or did not touch? Every herd
Of beasts, every man woman child our spoil and booty,
Captively free. Now, children, we will be very, very good.

Mattot, Num. 30:2 – 32:42

10. (Road map)

We were good as we had to be, mainly. We packed up one place
We went another, as orders came down from on high.
We crossed, in no great order, one desert waste
Upon another, learning or not, fumbling our way,
But keeping track. *Migdol. Marah. Twelve springs*
Of water at Eilim. The wilderness
Of Sin. Now comes the time of reckonings,
And mapping out, and staking claim: a fence
Goes up around our towns and settlements:
We cower behind the Assassin's Gate: and what good
And what refuge will come of it, and whence
Will come our help, now we are more afraid?
Encamped again in the wilderness of our strife,
Out in the open, in the midst of life.

Mase'ei, Num. 33:1-36:13

At the Summer Lake Club

He'd come in every weekday afternoon
To play the organ, a battered Hammond
He'd acquired years ago, like his repertoire—
Standards, mostly, "Ebb Tide" and "Caravan,"
Songs as out-of-date as the double-breasted
Suits he'd wear, thin and thready at the seams.
He was Charlie, our weekday entertainment,
Though Saturdays, when diners filled the room,
A modern trio pumped out cloying pop,
And Sunday brunch was piped-in classical—
Hindemith and Mozart, strains of Schubert
For a crowd decked-out in their Sabbath best.
I was the bartender that year, eager
To learn my trade and keep the patrons happy,
Just a kid adrift until that fall when
Grad school beckoned and I'd give up slinging
Drinks for Tennyson and Shakespeare.
Charlie would arrive and order a scotch:
"First things first," he'd say, then narrow his eyes
With pleasure as he drained his glass.
I never saw a man so hot for drink,
An act so lurid, so voluptuous,
We felt we had to turn away, though Pete,
Our Mexican maitre'd whose real name
Was Pedro, cut him off at three—no more.
The other two were measured out at five
And six PM, exactly one each hour.
At first I thought him crazy, just a bum
With nowhere else to go, a holdover
From the big bands blasting from my father's
78s. But the clientele enjoyed him,
And the ladies liked his patter when he
Wasn't drunk, flattering them with unctuous
Jokes, and leering coyly at the children.
"Hey, Charlie, you've got your head up your past!"
Someone shouted once, and Charlie
Slammed his fist on the organ, then glared

At the room: "Who said that!" he thundered,
"And what do you know about music?
I oughta leave." But Charlie stayed, because
Humiliation is only a step from pride.
I even grew to like him and his music—
The old organ wheezing at his touch, legs
Wobbling below to find the bass notes,
Bony shoulders swaying to the rhythm.
He was part of summer. Without him
Something might be missing, a treasured piece
Of the past, a piece of ourselves, floating off
Unnoticed to be swallowed in the haze
At mid-lake where boats would drift, and vanish.

Civil War in Seventh Period

It took us over an hour to seize McPherson's Ridge,
that *anvil*, our teacher rhapsodized,
which would break the hammer
of Lee's army. Apparently the Confederacy couldn't be defeated
without the help of metaphors.
Culp's Hill, Cemetery Hill, Seminary Ridge –
by Friday we were exhausted
from going up and down so many eminences,
Peach Orchard Salient, Little Round Top.
It was up to us, every day,
between 11:15 a.m. and 12:05 p.m.. to free the slaves,
which was no small task
since the sun chose precisely that period
to find the backs of our necks.
In the middle of the Battle of Antietam it slipped inside our shirts
and worked its way down our legs
by the time we stormed Atlanta.
It made our eyelids heavy at the most inopportune moments.
While men at Cold Harbor sewed notes into their uniforms –
Daughter, remember me. Mother I'm sorry. June 3. I was killed –
we were falling asleep at our posts.
Vicksburg, Fredericksburg, Petersburg, Sharpsburg –
how could we keep all those burgs straight?
By the time we'd marched from Wilderness to Five Forks,
360,022 Union soldiers had given their lives
to their flag, 258,000 Rebels
to their flag, and it was already April
and our minds were on other things beside saving the Union.
Like Grant before Appomattox, Mr. Brengle paced the room,
but our thoughts were elsewhere
on the sun that caressed our faces as we drowsed
through The Terms of Surrender. Right before lunch
he made it clear that we were letting down Abraham Lincoln.
Our teacher's next favorite activity,
besides fighting the Civil War on the blackboard,
was making us ashamed to be fifteen and bored.

He knew who the real enemy of America was: boys
just like us throughout our troubled nation
allowing themselves to be distracted
by something insignificant as light.

In Memoriam

Tobias Schneebaum, 1922-2005

He was an adventurous guy. Even at Yaddo
In Saratoga, playing charades, he would do things
That provoked the other players to speak in
Whispers and look out the corners of their eyes.
I'm not gay, he would say, I'm a homosexual.
He was also a Jew, an artist, and a gossip, a
Delightful guy. One time he found himself
At a Catholic mission on the edge of the great
Amazonian rainforest, entertaining the
Brothers with caricatures and naughty suggestions,
And someone told him of the Arakamas.
They lived in the jungle and were cannibals
Allegedly. Schneebaum's name was Theodore,
Which he disliked. He changed it to Tobias
And insisted on the full pronunciation. If
Anyone said Toby, he would frown and make
A gasping noise and throw up the window, waving
The bad air out. Tobias decided to go looking
For the Arakamas. He packed a small knapsack
And walked south along the river for many days
Until around a bend he saw the natives standing
On the farther shore. He stopped on a sandbar and took
Off all his clothes. Then he held out his hands in
A friendly, half-supplicating gesture, and walked
Up to them. Months later he was still there,
Covered with paint, sleeping each night with a dozen
Lovers, eating human flesh to keep up his
Strength. Later he said it tasted like roast
Pork. And then he went to Borneo and did the
Same thing. Living in Asmat on the coast of
Irian Jaya, where he established a wonderful
Museum of native Indonesian art and
Culture. He began lecturing, he wrote books, he made
Drawings and paintings of native life, he became
Actually popular in our proud nation of armchair

Anthropologists. A documentary film was made,
Which was an ordeal for him. He wrote me letters
From New York and Peru, filled with acrimony
For the film-makers and their absurd demands.
He was always in pain from his legs, and finally he
Was diagnosed with Parkinson's. He could no
Longer answer my letters. Then a few days ago
He died. I saw his obit in the *Times*, and I felt
A sort of deflating gasp in my lungs, and I knew
As I had not before how lonely this life has
Become and is becoming. Tobias is gone,
And the hurricanes rage. Can anyone else
Become a real explorer in this dark time?

Pigs Advance as Organ-Transplant Factories for People

–Headline, *The Seattle Times*, October 22, 2002

Power to the people–
did I really yell it? And, going whole hog, *off the pig*!–
in my salad days, an organic
soybean eater, greenest of greenhorn transplants
from the suburbs, dying for a role in some advance
guard or other, AWOL from the knowledge factory.

I know I took a job in a donut factory,
like an old-time *narodnik*, "going to the people."
Better, I thought, than whoring for an advanced
degree, though I still felt complicit in my civilization's pig-
out. Chairman Mao had the poets making bricks, transplanting
rice, which earned him raves in the underground organs.

"I believe I have injured an organ,"
fibs the doomed grandmother in that factory
of existential yuks, Flannery O'Connor's transplanted
passion play, the one about the people
who get offed on their vacation. Her homespun Pyg-
malion, aka the Misfit, pumps spiritual advance-

ment from the barrel of a gun. My fiction class (advanced)
panned the plot (heavy-handed). A good cadaver organ's
hard to find, the *Times* explains–and look, a pig
has penned a spirited defense of factory
farm techniques. "I believe I have injured the people,"
blurts a shamefaced government, and orders a transplant,

stat. Facelift? Honey, save up for a cranium transplant.
I believe I have injured my planet. Your advances
underwhelm me. How come they say "the people"

when they mean the prosecutor? Don't go postal, organ-
ize. (First find where NAFTA's stashed the factories.)
The small-island child who loved the fried blood of pigs

now cooks with tofu, tempeh, TVP. PETA's pig
supporters gird for a melee with relatives of transplant-
ation hopefuls on Astroturf behind the bioethics factory.
It just gets so complicated. What means this verb "to advance?"
Do monkeys hit glass ceilings doing gigs with organ
grinders? That's the trouble with you people.

You toss some token pig a six-figure advance
for her saga of transplant hell; you gobble ribs, bacon, organ
meats. You hesitate: are women fetus factories or people?

Enkidu's Lament

(from "Lessons from Ancient Iraq")

It's the first warm day of spring.
The robins are back and the forsythia is blooming.
I'm reaching down to pick up the ball
for the little girl who kicked it here.
The sky is painfully blue.
I'm punished for the slightest emotion.
That "painfully" – I take it back
at the cost of an arm.
What's an arm? I ask.
I've got another for holding you.
Mistakes are measured here in body parts.
This air I breathe is thick with souls
that fill me with what they've lost.
Tempt me with excessive talk.
So few bodies remain, lingering at the stile,
forgetting their names.
My name is Enkidu, former wild man
of the steppes and friend of the king.
I would say nothing forever
if silence were forbidden.

Win Chinese Buffet

Nick and I were hungry—he'd been driving
all morning. The strip mall didn't look promising,
but the windows of Win Chinese Buffet were clean,

not greasy, which is our main eatery-choosing criteria
when we're on a long road trip. Inside, the food bar
glistened with all the usual glutinous sauces

and we each filled our plates. When Nick went
for a second heap of rice, a waiter came to refill
our water and asked me: *What kind of a guy*

is that guy? I blinked. *Happy?* I asked him,
meaning my husband loved Win's General Tso's
chicken. *Happy Korean?* he asked. And I got it.

No, I said, *Happy Filipino.* Oh, he said, very good.
I wanted to ask the waiter what kind of a guy he was,
but he was off with his pitcher, ice clinking,

to other tables. I wondered what kind of customers
he was serving, what kind of men, what kind of women,
what kind of kids. I guessed two little girls

were with their dad, who I guessed was divorced
since the girls were dressed up, not saying much, cutting
their egg rolls into small polite bites with forks and knives.

Nick came back with his rice, two construction workers
with beach ball bellies following behind. I wondered
what kind of Win family would open

their restaurant here, how they came to the states,
Columbia, SC in particular. Nick stretched, anticipating
the long afternoon of driving ahead. His shoulder

hurt, but I thought he said his soldier hurt, and it
was one of those times in our marriage that I wish
we could hit rewind, since I was sure what I heard

was right. I wondered what kind of general Nick
would be, probably not a very good one,
since he didn't like conflict and his soldier hurt.

General Tso, on the other hand, has been compared
to American Civil war leader Stonewall Jackson
as an inspiration to the soldiers under his command.

One of my favorite poems as a kid
was "The Land of Counterpane" by Robert Louis Stevenson,
who was the kind of kid who was sickly a lot,

which is the kind of kid I was, too.
I totally related to how he watched like a general
his "leaden soldiers go, with different uniforms

among the bedclothes..." Counterpane
was my first big vocabulary word–
initially I thought it had something to do with pain

since the little boy in the poem is playing in bed.
I remember guessing that counterpane
meant over-the-counter medicine.

Though I used a prescription inhaler, when I ran out
I could also get one at the drug store called Primatene Mist.
It tasted really bad, the spray usually winding up

as a puddle on the back of my tongue.
And what kind of a couple was that icy couple
across from us? Two well-dressed seniors,

the man dabbing his lips as though his napkin were cloth
not paper, the woman tapping her cigarette pack
on the table, signaling she was ready to go

and have a smoke in the parking lot.
They were restrained, on the edge of a dispute,
I could tell. And I wondered whose families had once

fought whose, how we were now all brought together
in Win's by this plentiful chowmein. Nick's fortune
said that his happiness was intertwined with his outlook

on life. Mine said it was a good time to look
at what has been familiar in a new way.
The fortunes also listed lucky numbers

and a special "Learn Chinese" scroll across the bottom.
We thought it a good sign our words mirrored each other's.
Nick's: Yi-Tong, one bucket. Mine: Tong-Yi, to agree.

Returning to the Ravens

For Madeleine & Joel

One April in Ketchikan, amid the politics
of Alaska and the exotica of large birds,
I found myself amused by the posturing
and strutting of ravens, the all-day-long
whimsy of their short flights, the way
they'd blacken the cedars,
then suddenly return to the streets.
Everything they did suggested mischief.
Then there were the eagles, fierce
and humorless, as the efficient often are,
up there at such a distance
their reputation could never diminish.
I felt I was watching privilege,
the advantages of birth, and would return
each day to where the ravens gathered,
happy to see their I've-got-a-secret smirks.
No doubt it was time to go home,
let the birds be birds, without choice.
The morning I left, raucous gulls circled
white fishing boats in the harbor.
Democrats of a catch not theirs,
they made no distinction between leftovers
and meals achieved by headlong dives
and perfect, clean entries. All appetite,
they just wanted what they wanted.
A light rain was falling, everything gray.
Among plenitude, the gulls squabbled,
the sky undulant with their trashy beauty.

Army Men

1

Isaac, for whom I prayed, is back from Iraq.
My poetry student three years ago, before he left
he said, *I joined ROTC for the scholarship,*
why else? The Marines made him a pacifist.

He's different now. One eyelid twitches,
small as waterbugs' ripples on still waters.
They're crazy, they love to kill each other...
He picks up his spoon, lifts soup

but doesn't eat. *We slept on the ground,*
didn't wash...we drove around, filled in
wherever they needed us.
He starts to eat but lets the spoon drop.

When Katrina hit I got my 100-gallon
water jug and drove on down to Biloxi.
We lost it all but I was home
in the wreckage and death and nothing.

Just like Iraq, it was great... The muscles of his face
tighten, the way roadkill bare their teeth
as the flesh dries. *I'm not a pacifist anymore.*
I've done things that I'm ashamed of.

2

I'd like to say I don't understand him, but I do.
You do what you gotta do, he says.
When I was small, my Army father showed me
how to kill a man:

surprise him from behind,
wrap your arm around his neck,

and then *Crack!* he'd pretend to do it to me,
push up on the jaw, and *There goes the neck bone.*

For years, I dreamed my father
lurking through darkness with his billyclub,
sneaking up behind, then *crack!*-ing bad Koreans.
Or hacking at jungles, guarding prisoners.

Or locked up in a Quonset hut, chained
and tortured for secrets, with only a bowl
and a concrete floor. I was sure
they would find a twin for my father

and send him to Japan to join us.
My mother would be fooled, accept his gifts
of garnets and pearls, never know
he was locked up somewhere.

3

One photograph, and others: My father
in Korea, hair slicked back,
skinny and kind, the science geek
in his khaki winter uniform and glasses.

And on the internet today:
faces of little girls
eaten with white phosphorus.

4

My father never talked about his wars.
I never saw on his face that tight
jumpy snarl with which Isaac seems to glance
into brutal efficiency, into someone screaming.

But my mother said, when she picked him up
at the Omaha train station, Christmas '45,
she found him alone on a bench
at the far end of the room, huddled over,

28

head in his hands. She said they just looked
at each other for a while, not speaking,
silence gathered around them.
I asked her what was wrong.

If you don't know, she said, *I can't tell you.*
And she told me it took months
for the telegram to reach her,
the telegram he sent to let her know he was returning,

because he addressed it, simply: *Home Street.*

5

What do I know? Not much.

As a child, I leapt to my feet
whenever I heard "The Star-Spangled Banner,"
climbed from the car to stand at attention
at Taps while they folded the flag.

In the basement in the '50's, Pennsylvania,
my father kept his billyclub. Somewhere,
his rifles and pistols. In his bureau,
the dogtags, the medals for marksmanship.

He wrote us stories about a dog named Pinkelfritz
and a dog named Fritzpinkel
and a cat named Kitty BlueRibbon, from Seoul.
He shined his shoes every Sunday morning.

At the end of World War II
he screamed, once, in his honeymoon sleep.
But my mother told me that. She also said,

on the road to Manila
he could smell the bodies burning.

Crows

You came with your dark hats,
fringed shawls, gifts–
armloads of flowers and grief.

You came with twigs,
muddy houses, ashes
smeared on your cheeks.

You came with your broken clocks,
loud warnings. You came
with your wisdom,

but your wisdom was air.
You came with your umbrellas open
despite the sun,

and the sun shone in the feathers
of your wings held close
to your bodies. You came with your offering,

the corpses of mice and birds,
bundles of bones,
and the bones were bloody,

and bloody were your beaks
and talons ticking
the long black table.

Video Game

You ride the joystick
until the beam locks in
your target. Then
you press the button
that delivers the payload.

The palaces buckle.
Emerald domes
shatter before they hit
ground, green
stones glinting.

The tents where the poor
live collapse.
Amidst the debris
are the smoking roads.

Orange flames billow
through the countryside.
You can almost feel
the heat under your fingertips.
Colorful balloons burst

like noiseless screams.
You close your eyes
and enter the clouds,
proud of your success,

but your signal breaks up,
and everything turns
to dust, air and rain,
as you hurtle toward a white
wall that won't give.

Prayer For My Unborn Niece Or Nephew

Today, November 28th, 2005, in Pittsburgh, Pennsylvania,
I am staring at my hands in the common pose
of the hungry and penitent, studying
the emptiness therein, where I see
my sister-in-law days from birthing
the small thing which will erase,
in some sense, the mystery of my father's departure;
their child will emerge with ten fingers,
and toes, howling, and his mother will hold
his gummy mouth to her breast and the stars
will hang above them and not one bomb
will be heard through that night. And my brother will stir,
waking with his wife the first few days, and he will run
his long fingers along the soft terrain of his child's skull
and not once will he cover the child's ears
or throw the two to the ground and cover them
from the blasts. And this child will gaze
into a night which is black and quiet.
She will pull herself up to her feet
standing like a buoy in wind-grooved waters,
falling, and rising again, never shaken
by an explosion. And her grandmother
will watch her stumble through a park or playground,
will watch her sail through the air on swings,
howling with joy, and never once
will she snatch her from the swing and run
for shelter because again, the bombs are falling.
The two will drink cocoa, the beautiful lines
in my mother's face growing deeper as she smiles
at the beautiful boy flipping the pages of a book
with pictures of dinosaurs, and no bomb
will blast glass into this child's face, leaving
the one eye useless. No bomb will loosen the roof,
crushing my mother while this child, four, sees
plaster and wood and blood where once his nana sat.

This child will not sit with his nana, killed by a bomb,
for hours. I will never drive across two states
to help my brother bury my mother this way. To pray
and weep and beg this child to speak again.
She will go to school with other children,
and some of them will have more food than others,
and some will be the witnesses of great crimes,
and some will describe flavors with colors, and some
will have seizures, and some will read two grade
levels ahead, but none of them will tip their desks
and shield their faces, nor watch as their teacher
falls out of her shoes, clinging to the nearest child.
This child will bleed
and cry and curse his living parents
and slam doors and be hurt and hurt again. And she will feel
clover on her bare feet. Will swim in frigid waters.
Will climb trees and spy cardinal chicks blind
and peeping. And no bomb will kill this child's parents.
No bomb will kill this child's grandparents. No bomb
will kill this child's uncles. And no bomb will kill
this child, who will raise to his mouth
some small morsel of food of which there is more
while bombs will fall from a sky like dust
brushed from the hands of a stupid god and children
whose parents named them will become dust
and their parents will drape themselves in black
and dream of the tiny mouths which once reared
to suckle or gasp at some bird sailing by
and their tears will make a mud which will heal nothing,
and today I will speak no word
except the name of that child whose absence
makes the hands of her parents shiver, a name
which had a meaning.
As will yours.

after Aracelis Girmay

Samaritan

...going down from Jerusalem to Jericho...
–Luke 10: 30-37

Just outside the city walls, yet again I came upon a person, this one

in his artisan's booth – it was framed of weathered dark thick beams of wood built against the ancient stone that belonged to everyone

and no one,

he was standing at the open entrance under a sign that announced only his name,

in some language or other that I knew and didn't know, "Tigerman,"

and in fact I wondered at first if somehow he

was a tiger – his peculiar strong bare arms were striped by some inconceivable feral gene or affliction of the skin, and his round face

had an almost feline configuration of the nose and mouth, or seemed to have, his assistant,

I thought it was, at first, wore a belt of chain that was in fact a leash attached to a brutal spike

that had been driven decisively into the stone back wall of the booth, and his misshapen head

could not help with anything, and his right hand was withered, his legs were stout and slow, but at the limit of his leash and being

he smiled and stayed near the tiger man, his guardian,

who constructed and offered for sale to the occasional tourist

his small sculptures of black wrought iron, twisted and bent to resemble somewhat abstract figures

of animals and men and women,

unlike any such art of making I had ever before seen, and then a grandfather wearing the faded uniform of a soldier,

with hair and short beard still strikingly black and with black eyes – I thought perhaps he was an Akkadian or Kurd, a former dragoman or a Babylonian or Afghani

who had fled west – stopped to watch the artisan

set up a small side space using two more of the heavy wood beams – evidently a kind of temporary annex where he could create his symbols

and which he would break down again each day after he

had made and sold a few pieces of this craft – and the older man, the stranger,

without speaking bent down quickly behind the tiger man

to volunteer his remaining strength to help lift the next beam, one end of which the tiger man

had hefted already above his head, and the old man lifted his end high but the tiger man

was startled by this unrequested aid behind him, had not understood what wordlessly his fellow creature –

perhaps some former artisan himself, or former cat – was doing for him

and because of his own sudden surprised movement in response to that of the old foreigner

the lifeless beam slipped from the older man's still strong hands striking him in the head and knocking him down and the tiger man with alarm and anger heaved the whole evil

beam to one side and leapt to undo too late the wound but the casualty

lay awkwardly pushing himself

backwards in the dirt and away, trying to lift himself with one arm,

not bleeding but confused and harmed, and a graceful, unperturbed woman

came out from among the hurrying, burdened, mostly oblivious pedestrians,

she knelt and when she noticed that his black eyes seemed to see with a different gaze or not to see at all, she

pressed him down, her touch urging him to remain very still – until, I supposed, rescuers

could arrive. And then the simple ward

of the tiger man, fighting his unyielding leash in order to see, to get near him

who was hurt, began to make an anguished sound that I

am unable to describe, and I stood listening in awe as from his mouth, from his head, from his poor body,

there came a sound that filled the street around us

as the leashed man was reaching toward the fallen elder, filled with the need to help, would-be Samaritan –

but one unable ever to know to breathe into the child

pulled from the sea or to know how to nurse the traveler

who has been attacked or to protect the mother

walking home at too late an hour, unable to save from error

that hapless citizen who stubbornly, with the ballot before him, invites the rule of his tyrant.

And in my mind

I rushed away. Perhaps finally weeping, as the tiger man tried to help, to watch over, to hold close, to calm, his good ward,

who was tearing at himself in his pain of compassion.

Drongo

Not even when she was diagnosed; or when they stilled her sobbing
with the anesthesia, then wheeled her in; or when she was released,
without her bladder but, instead, a bag
that turned this intimate alchemizing inside-out...not even
then could Evan cry for his mother, although the sorrow
was honestly in him, in his head, in a lump up there
like a portion of salt-pork that a sailor might gnaw:
it was private, it wanted to stay in the dark and fester.
When he finally did cry, a grade-Z cheese-o-rama movie did it:
lushly weepy background music, and a noble band
of refugees attempting to clamber doggedly over a mountain
(and against the oath of a dragon-riding sorcerer of the kind
whose faux-Shakespearian rantings dominate such films).
It was, he told me, as the few remaining members of that troop

descended safely to the mountain's farther side, and the sun
and the synthesized orchestral overflowing combined into one
sublingual emotional cue the size of the entire theater (after all,
a movie screen is up to 80% of our visual field) that he yielded
to this sanction, and he poured out woe, enormous unpluggable
torrents of woe, as if he were an industry that was hired
to produce enough surplus tears for export
to the woe-impoverished rest of the world. "I sat there,"
he said, "until an usher led me outside like a five-year-old."
This is why heroic grief is commemorated in gods with the bodies
of stars and cosmic vacuum, in a sky we've made our storyboard:
because we also burn, we struggle mightily with the void,
and with the glory of light and with its disappearance: and we need
those stars, the way we need the hypershlock of Hollywood:

to give our hearts their accurate, correlative expression. It
was true, his mother *is* trying to climb the world's
most perilous mountain—only inside herself; and there
she fights her dragon. Its great hunger: for her bladder only
seemed to tease that appetite. And true, too, when the sorcerer
—the dark force of that movie—toppled down a ravine, to the pyrotechnic
special effects of his death, it made a moment
when each member of the audience felt emptied of whatever
individual misfortune tortured him or her: symbolically,
what plagued them had been driven from the village;
they were left clean. It's so good to have a Jew to blame, to whip
into the borderlands; a woman to mark with a scarlet A;
a messiah to die for your sins; a spry factotum to leap and take
the bullet intended to splatter your chest. A lovely vision

of this is current in the markets of Hyderabad, in India:
the locals believe they can buy "a black drongo,
a crow-like bird," and whisper their problems into its ear,
and release...as it flies away, the trouble flies away.
A rougher version is in Orwell's *1984*: the state knows
it can only break the will of Winston Smith if he'll betray the one
he loves: and when he's threatened with a cage of rats
attached to his face, indeed he screams out "Do it to Julia!"
She becomes his drongo. Once, I visited the hospital
with Evan. In the room across the hall, I saw a woman
—she was maybe fifty, black, and on her knees
beside the bed that held her father—whisper loud enough
for me to hear, "Lord, let some white man die instead." And no,
it wasn't pretty; but then neither was her circumstance.

A 15-year-old Indian girl called Savitri was admitted to hospital suffering from tiny stones that emerged from the corners of her eyes. Said Dr. Ragho Saran, "Stones are formed due to the high level of calcium in the body. But they are usually found in the gall bladder and kidney. This is the first time I have ever heard of stones coming out of the eyes."

-arranged from *The Fortean Times*

If I thought true enough, could every one arrive in the shape
of its specific heartache?–a house with a hole in the middle;
a teething ring; a knife on the bed.... And feel free
to put in an order for yours. Because I need to believe
I suffer with this purpose: I need assurance that the ocean
of our misery is channeled as a hardness
through these two pink gates, the better
to be eloquent. For you. Because, admit it, there have been days
when the stone of contempt was heavy in you–and yet
you couldn't say it; the stone of the fear of death was a blockage
inside–and yet you had no public voice. The stones,
the mountain of stones, the filibustering stones, but not
one outward sign. Well...here I am. And here they are:
compacted;   aphoristic.

The Window

The dogs of war whimper just beyond the glass pane frightened,
as usual, by their own confusion and meaninglessness.

How not to feel shame at the absence of shame?

In the steady progression of days, patience.
In the regular decline of the sun, powerlessness.

I cannot see what you see until I fear what you fear,
love what you love, honor what you honor.

The window is open.

Listen, Friends

We live like barnacles clinging to rocks
swept night and day by tides of love.

Let's not waste time asking if war is ever good.

With each flood curiosity, desire, ecstatic action.
With each ebb suspicion, dread, armored solitude.

What stands between us and what we want?
What could we want except to live as love,

fluid and in motion, unafraid and eternal?
Listen, Friends, this drunkenness needs no wine.

When did we last kiss as if it were our last kiss?

Ghazal: Across the Street

Three cops – what are they waiting for across the street ?
I'd make some quip, but you're not with me, or across the street.

Sedentary traveler, facing my window
blinds rise on provinces I still explore across the street.

Who'll move into the newly-renovated two-bedroom
flat (opposite mine) on the fourth floor across the street ?

I bought *Le Monde* late afternoons at the newsstand
replaced by one more pricey menswear store across the street.

I still knot a scarf to stand in the bakery line
– you teased me, for caring what I wore across the street.

Fat drops fall. Shoppers huddle under the awning
till the bus comes. It starts to pour across the street.

I write « you, » shorthand for one more absence.
A motorcycle revs up with a roar across the street.

The bus heads eastward with its sodden passengers
out of my vision like a metaphor across the street.

Now the cops – two boys, one girl, not thirty –
seem less inquisitive than jocular across the street.

The rain has stopped as quickly as it started
but there's no news-fix anymore across the street.

If they imagine women forget dead babies
in those countries, they don't imagine war across the street.

A window opens like a book on evening,
Light silvers grillwork on a door across the street.

Pollution gives the sky to feral pigeons.
They coo over more territory than before across the street.

Above the frieze of chimneys, antennas and window-gables,
swallows in V-formation used to soar across the street.

Gospel

Hatred is wise beyond its years.
Hatred is intent, clever, and patient,

sophisticated and implacable.
When hatred enters the garden

it consumes every rose and cabbage,
every ear of corn, every hollyhock.

Hatred is diligent, it is cellular,
it is replicable. If we cut off

hatred's head, ten new murders
grow from the pod of its head.

Flower Shop

Stepping in from the street,
the heat would drop away
and a sigh of greenery
announce itself.

First it was “Bill’s Flowers” lettered in blue
on a white panel truck.
Bill was a blond model-type,
something short of 6 feet tall,
and skinny in a tight jeans kind of way.

And then he was gone. Guys were flying out
the windows quick with some new death blow
eventually named AIDS. Did Bill ever look sick?
Who knew what to look for,
We were just shopping for flowers.

It was a place to order up a special bouquet,
pink *Heliconia* and ginger blossoms, maybe.
Thai orchids with sweet baby faces,
pricey but spectacular. Always something
exotic highlighting the beautiful window displays.

Paul took over after Bill died. The truck got repainted
with a little pinstripe below the name “Paul’s Plants.”
I was buying more vases and single stems of things.
I liked to wander from room to room,
the best part of shopping there,
moving through the flower shop’s damp and tactile air.

Now Paul is dead, too—his meds never worked.
The truck reads “Green & Co.”
Letters in a ceramic lime,
and right at the end of the line,
two little daisies punctuating it.

I don't know Green yet. Maybe he's a survivor.
Maybe he's young. He's pretty great, though,
with the window displays. My friend Maria
thinks he has a background in set design.
All of the workers have stayed on and so has
that beautiful glade of rooms.

Where They Were

For Anne Marie Macari

They were in Sweden, in Paris.
In Mexico City. In Venezuela.
The thirty thousand, the however
many had not answered
the latest roll call.

So said the general. The colonels.
Some lieutenants. Even the few
cadets of the Army School I knew.
Gone to Denmark. To Barcelona.
Zipping through Rome in little

scooters. Sending postcards. Asking
their poor mothers for more money.
Who were the mothers in the Plaza?
Covering up for the gone.
Making a wretched, wretched noise.

I went from thirteen to eighteen
eating the white sour bread of lie,
and the way we sang bland rock 'n roll
quieted the whispers, kept us
light-blue and innocent.

They were in Lima, crowding Madrid,
smoking *la frula* of Amsterdam,
on the long solitary walk of exile;
alive but skinless with nostalgia,
alive and breathing the rare foreign air.

So said the majors. And the beautiful,
immaculate Navy cadets on deck,
and the police. The news anchormen
tut-tutting the rumors, patting their gilded
hair. Were they homesick, the gone?

And we awoke and were so heavy
with the black-green years. So much mud
to go through, sifting for little things,
an earring, one of the wrist bones, a name.
We had been celibate for the motherland.

There was such a roar instead of singing.
The news came from abroad in empty envelopes.
The full things were the ditches where
the gone were entwined and known only
to themselves and each tangled other.

The cadets wore royal blue crossed
with red silk sashes. They could dance.
Nobody knew how we had come to own
so much hatred. Nobody knew. Nobody.
Nunca supimos nada.

First published in Logos Journal *(on line), Fall 2005.*

AP Photo: Two Rwandan Women Reunited in a Church in Kabiza, 1997

All around you, the green
is still your green: tea plantations
in ruins, dead banana trees.
The soil red from its rusted self,
looking like powdered blood.

Your peasant hands splayed
and knotted, headcloth leaning
on headcloth, the better to bring
the embroidered blouses tight
to one another. Who knew
there was this much to lose?
That little wealth measured in water
gourds would leave such holes?

If your neighbor is not there to sing
while your menses drown you,
to bind your baby to her back
for today, the birds of carrion
might just as well be feeding
off the sorrow around your hips.

If her mortar and pestle do not grind
down the mist over the landscape,
you cannot cook or sew.
These two years apart have had
the length of all the bolts of cloth.
You don't know a measure for this:

the dead covered in lime,
the voice gone away with the song birds,
the body that becomes its own graveyard.

On the brick floors of a church in Kabiza
you find each other right on the brink
of vanishing, and you cling on to the heart
of the day, your wailing dusted
in hope. This dance of reunion has just
the one step, and a long note hangs on air:
Friend, friend, friend.

Shadow: An Assay

Mostly we do not think of, even see you,
shadow,
for your powers at first seem few.

Why command "Heel," ask "Sit,"
when before the thought is conceived,
you are already there?

True that sometimes you run ahead, sometimes behind,
that *early* and *late*,
to you, must be words of the deepest poignance:
for while inside them, you are larger than you were.

Midday drives you to reticence, sulking, a silence
I have felt many times as well.

You came with me to Krakow, Glasgow, Corfu.
Did you enjoy them?
I never asked.
Though however close my hand came to the table,
you were closer, touching before my tongue
the herring and cheeses, the turpentine-scented retsina.

Many times I have seen you sacrifice yourself
without hesitation,
disentangling yourself like Anna Karenina from her purse
before passing under the train wheels inside your own thoughts.
Like art though, you are resilient: you rose again.

Are you then afterlife, clutterless premonition?
You shake your head as soon as I do—
no, we think not.
Whatever earth I will vanish silently into, you also will join.

You carry, I have read,
my rages, fears, and self-regard.
You carry, I have read, my unrevealed longings,
and the monster dreamed as a child, tongueless and armless.
Your ordinary loneliness I recognize too as my own.

When you do not exist,
I have gone with you into darkness,

as the self of a former life
goes into the self that was tortured and beaten
and does not emerge again as it was,
though given a clean shirt to leave in, given pants and new shoes.

For this too is shadow, and mine,
however unspoken:
though you are tongueless, and armless, you harm.
Your inaction my own deepest failure, close by my side.

You who take nothing, give nothing, instruct me,
that my fate may be more than yours—

The hour is furious, late.
Your reach, horizontal, distant, leans almost forgiving,
almost indistinguishable from what it crosses.

We Lived Happily During the War

and when they bombed other people's houses, we

protested
but not enough, we opposed them but not

enough. And we kept repeating that grand moment:

a president saluting a flag on an enormous ship.

I knew I did not say much. I was
in my bed, around my bed America

was falling: invisible house by invisible house by invisible house.

I took a chair outside and watched the sun.

In the sixth year
of a disastrous reign in the house of money

in the street of money, in the city of money, in the country
of money, our great country of money, we (forgive us)

lived happily during the war.

– *For Eleanor Wilner*

Brother

"You must speak not only of great devastation
but of caterpillars in the yellow grass!"

I heard this not from a great philosopher or thinker
but from my brother Tony,

who could do four haircuts in thirteen minutes
with his eyes closed, reciting our National Anthem by heart.

"You must drink red wine and naked sing all night.
Unite, caterpillars of the Earth!."

and he played the accordion out of tune in the country
where the only musical instrument is the door.

"You must speak not only of great devastation"
so said my brother, who could not write or read

but spent his days covered in other people's hair.

Not In Our Names

for Mairead Corigan Maguire

See her at the table in the light, her pen
writing the letter he will read when he's grown

It will not be easy for you to refuse to kill
It will take all your courage to walk unarmed

Another table, more light, my hand, the pen.
The market is free: I'm free to buy them a gun

or would they like a tank? A plane, a mine, a bomb?
Or I could buy oranges to eat on the way to prison.

Our names are the aria of water down a falls.
Our names are the thunder of light across a page.

My name can buy a child, naked, running, burning.
Will he drop their bomb or walk to prison singing?

Either way his mother will still love him.
Here, take half. I don't want to eat this orange alone.

Bulldozer Sestina: Rafa, 2004

...a day overdetermined by Americans.
Marilyn Hacker

The girl: Rula Abu Abid. Her doll
Larla has no head. Rula rocks the body,
its white gown. *We took each other's hands*
and ran, waving white headscarves. Rula's face:
find the missing piece, put back the broken
doll, the broken house, this broken day

dozers ground to rubble. Perfidy
is all they own. One pillow and this doll
their worldly goods. Down the street a broken
sewing machine. *The temple of the body*
is our dwelling place: now turn and face
the wall. Grandfather, let's look. Her hand

takes his. Hand in hand, we say. One hand
can take another hand, or not. (The day
aches: weeps beside its coffin.) A face
that turns away is like a slap. Her doll
has no face. Can't cry. Sadness, the body's
task, goes on and on next to a broken

wheelchair. *(This is my body broken*
for you.) They call Ariel The Dozer. His hands
are mine, and yours. He dwells inside his body
\as we do. Knows sadness. Longs each day
for light, for bread. For love. He'd put her doll's
head back if he were able. We are the face

of god (yes, lower case,) and we must face
each other and ourselves, and choose: a broken
bowl? A bowl that's whole? Rula's doll
without a head, or with? Another's hand—

or no one's hand? We choose and choose. One day
the light packs up and goes. We sing the body

electric and we weep. How now body
forth the kiss of peace? Her mother's face:
don't you have children? The hungry day
goes begging, holding in its hands a broken
bowl. One onion in her mother's hand,
the clothes they're wearing. One pillow. One doll,

no head. Rula's doll is dead. Her body
puts its face in its hands. Bless broken June,
this Tuesday. Rafa. Down. Bow down. Shalom.

Warnock Street, Philadelphia.1998

Mechanic and Hill Streets, southside Bethlehem, Pa. 1998

North Broad, near Parrish Street, Philadelphia. 1997

York and Clarion Streets, Philadelphia 1998

"Honest Lou's Pest Control." North Broad Street, Philadelphia. 1997

Rolling Mills and Coke Works. Bethlehem Steel Corp. Bethlehem, Pa. 1990

Inaugural

We started in the dark,
four crammed into the green Ford,
its rack and pinion steering bad
so we hawed in the wind
as we passed our bag of apples
and sang our way to DC
the day of his anointing.
Joined the human stream winding
around the stone courthouse –
supremely empty. No one opened a hose,
no one fired rubber bullets,
for this was democracy – we walked,
hoarse and sodden, lifting up signs and puppets
for one another all day in raw January rain –
and saw many passing the other way
in black Stetsons, in minks draped to the pavement.
They sneered as they walked past in their boots,
faces smooth and satisfied.
The bullies' feast was beginning.

Rouen, 1431

Once, as I lay in their filthy cell, pants laced
tight under my tunic, both knees
drawn to my breast — that was how I slept —
the guard's mouth gone slack, I rode
his snorting breath back to Les Tourelles.
Smelled gunpowder, felt it exploding
with sharp cracks, heard the wounded screaming
as I helped raise a scaling-ladder
against the redoubt, above us small axes,
maces, naked fists, yet my men climbing.
I was armored in full plate, except my head,
and the English archer found his mark between
my neck and shoulder. His arrow pierced
my flesh to its depth and came out
through my back. Its force flung me backward.
In the dream I was afraid again and wept,
Catherine not yet with me, as they stuffed
my wound with cotton, olive oil, bacon grease —
no anodyne. The pain came back to me
and almost woke me, and I saw the judges'
seals, thick red wax hardening on their paper,
before I saw her light and heard her voice.

The Long Goodbye

They stood outside the sliding doors
at the Boston Airport, two men,
one in traveling slacks and soft
leather shoes, the other in beach shorts
and scuffs, the flight delayed, twilight
cloaking the few young trees, swallows
swarming through the pinkish haze.
They spoke in whispers, heads close,
hunched over their small terrier
who squirmed from one set of arms
to the other, their mouths damp
with dog kisses, giggling, their long
fingers touching beneath her thick fur.
I watched from my bench as they
played out their protracted goodbye,
and missed my husband, my daughter,
our own drooling dogs and sleepy cat,
and when one of them looked up
and my eyes locked with his I was
shocked to see him stagger back- as if
he had been shot- away from the man
he so clearly loved, the dog held
like a child between them, step back
hard on the pavement, slipping a little
on a dirty orange rind dropped
near the trashcan, catching himself,
reaching one arm out to steady
his slight body on the newspaper stand.
I slid my eyes to the gravel
as if I had been the one to strike a match
and touch it to a spilled river of kerosene
pooling at their feet, as if behind my eyes
was every pair of eyes to have caught them
like this: naked in public, undefended,
then condemned them with a sneer,

a fist, a string of spit and curses, a rusty
pipe wrench, a cracked baseball bat
raised and shaking above their heads.
These men had stood before me
in the dusky air, their faces
open as roses, and I watched them
fold up, turn their backs, and walk away,
the glass doors wheezing closed
behind their fallen shoulders. It was
getting cold, dark. I was shivering
in my skin. Oh Lord,
what have we done to love?

Poem in the Manner of Guillaume Apollinaire

All right people listen up
I've got my marbles and my balls
I speak three languages am in decent shape
though wounded in the war what war
the last war though we didn't call it that
we called it the struggle who's we
we were friends and we threatened
the law-and-order crowd with visions
of a vast and strange new planet
of anarchy at the Louvre
but we weren't really your enemies
we just fell in love with the rhetoric
of the great boundary the unlimited future
go right ahead laugh I don't mind
it's nearly midnight the day is nearly over
and so is my youth I don't want
your pity just your money hand it to me
slowly and no false moves or I'll shoot

67

Migration South

Early morning along the river, animals pulsing
    but motionless—

like the Indigo Bunting resting its small blue body
    on a stalk of sorghum,

its head turned west in contemplation. All day
    hiking, canoeing, finding

what we could—a Jesus Lizard, crowned, with feet
    so fast it could walk on water

if it weren't frozen there trying to look
    like a stick, or the Spider Monkey

leaping between trees, arms and legs splayed wide
    overhead so it seemed

held still in space. That night, exhausted, I dimmed
    the lights, relieved to be alone,

as if I hadn't been able to think all day with
    so much life around me, till

in my half-sleep I heard rough wing-beats, not bird

but a harder rasping, and turned to face a cockroach size
    of a flattened hen's egg

scurrying behind a cabinet. Up in the thatched roof
    I imagined colonies of insects

watching over me, invisible multitude,
    and who was I to question them?

Who was I with my binoculars and books?

Not the Hissing Roach or Dusky Antbird, not
  a shelled thing with wings

that clicked when it moved, but a frightened
  creature of the north,

out of her habitat, no feeble quills on my back,
  no gliding from the tree,

just that same falling and falling again, startled

into my bed, into my own featherless skin. Overhead:
  clouds of tiny creatures,

the eyes of roaches, moths, broken arm
  of the bat, or a bird

trapped in the peaked roof, frantic for release.

Ants

An endless trail of leaf-cutter ants passed
before our feet and our guide Luis

told me how one had sliced
his skin in the cradle

between his thumb and second finger,
and how long it took to heal.

And like the temples and palaces
of Tikal I could imagine being

cut into some mosaic of myself, broken
by the ants into small bits

of green and brown and carried piecemeal
over the grass, my life

given over to a love of nothing in particular,
a scattering; I don't know how

he got to the subject of the milky way,
a road in the middle

parting the white silk of space, as if

the ants led there, through the trees,
down to earth,

then back up—all those small green
trapezoids of grief

filling the void—or why I remembered
suddenly, what it felt like to kiss,

how we could dissolve ourselves that way,
practicing through

our mouths for the next life, as the stones

on the temples so slowly and thoroughly
pressed against each other,

as the heat and dampness pressed

my eyelids and drummed

my chest. So much love ruining us,
as we are meant

to be ruined. The frame
collapsing. My hand raised toward

your face, your eyes

closing.

Not All of Me

Non omnis moriar multaque pars mei
~Horace

Early morning broken down
station wagon on 23rd Street, fender askew.

Rain about to fall,
trash spilling out of the wire baskets,

two men at the corner arguing baseball.
Upstairs I find messages

that I read and read again—
a salty grief coming through my skin—

last night's poison, last night's dream?
A poet friend died in his sleep, the war goes on,

a hurricane tore through the South.
Inside me an ocean is thickening.

Non omnis moriar, I remember,
taste of the earth in my mouth.

Rant Inspired by Frank Rich, "We Do Not Torture" and Other Funny Stories

New York Sunday Times, Op-Ed, Nov. 13, 2005

G. W.: *"Father, I cannot tell a lie."*
G. W. B.: *"Father, I cannot tell the truth."*

Lies lies lies lies lies.
You lie you lie you lie you lie you lie.
You lie he lies she lies they lie you lie.
You torture you torture you torture you torture you lie.

You torture you lie you torture you lie you lie.
Guantánamo Guantánamo Guantánamo Guantánamo you lie.
Abu Ghraib Abu Ghraib Abu Ghraib Abu Ghraib you lie.
Testing testing testing your weapons you lie.

Burn the people and not their clothing you lie.
Fallujah staring with phosphorous eyes you lie.
Thousands dead and thousands more will die.
You torture you burn you profit you lie you lie.

March of the Penguins

The editor of *National Review* urged [Young Republicans] to see the movie because it promoted monogamy. A widely circulated Christian magazine said it made "a strong case for intelligent design" —*The New York Times,* 9/13/05

What the hell are they going to do now
with the libidinous bluebird, who lines up
a couple of extra girlfriends every summer,
not to mention the evil house wrens —
don't be fooled by their cheery little calls,
they have up to five mates at a time!
I won't even mention the gay rabbits
we had once, in love with one another's ears,
etc., and even now my old friend Walter may be
declaiming how God planted dinosaur bones
to test the faith of Christians with the appearance
of evolution, thereby demonstrating once again
we are the first country to pass from barbarism
to decadence without an interlude, and as for
"intelligent design," even Britney Spears
wouldn't drop her eggs
at 70 below.

Two Arias From "Death and the Powers"

From the libretto for *Death and the Powers: A Robot Pageant*, with music by composer Tod Machover, commissioned by the Opera of Monte Carlo, premiere scheduled for Fall 2007.

The robots, as instructed by Human Creators in the remote Organic Age, perform the drama of Simon Powers, a billionaire who means to become immortal by having his consciousness become software–leaving behind the "meat machine" of the body. He intends to take his family along with him, but his beloved daughter resists the idea, for reasons both personal and political.

I. MORE

Don't talk about enough!
Enough is never enough!

Ask any body *How much money*
Would be enough for you?
Just about every body at any
Level, says double:
To double what they have
Or double what they make.

If they are ever able
To get it, then–they want
Double again.

What's enough being alive?
Why does the crushed bug
Keep waving a leg? That wave
Is for more, more more.

Forever doesn't matter.
Enough is not good enough.
What matters is *more*.

Get it and then you will beg
For more life again.

Forever is not the point.
More is what you want.

And if you think you've got
Three score years and ten
Then what you want is not
To outlive the sun,
But a hundred and forty—more!

Forever is not the point.
All that matters is more.
Don't talk about enough,
There's no such thing—
What you want is more:
All of life is intent
On more, more, more.

II. BAD MEAT

I appear to you one more time,
Dear Miranda, to explain

That I tried to help the world
Once, but the animal is defective.

It's not the poor or the starving
That hold you back. It's yourself—I know:

I tried to help the world too,
But it's in us, the problem is in us.

We evolved as meat, to love fat and sugar;
Once that was good, but now it is fatal.

We evolved as flesh, to want sex all the time;
Once that was good, but now it is only trouble.

We evolved as muscle, to want to make war;
Once that was good, but now it is lethal.

Our fat and sugar are killing us,
Our sweetness and abundance

Kill us, and lead us to famine
Bigger McMuck, Thicker Sweet Shake.

Sexier Shaking the Sweetness,
Smarter Weapons for Meat.

Meat wants Meat, Meat wants Sweet,
Sweats for the Sweets and the Meets–

Now there's no help but evolving
Out of the Meat, and into the system.
It isn't the Many and the Few–
It's yourself, it's you!

Come! Into the world of light!

Away from the bondage of meat!
Away from the wars and the sweat!

Pantoum

The gates were closing and the time was late
in spite of our efforts in the car,
our suitcases packed, our coats tossed off,
goodbyes said, or not to be said

in spite of our efforts in the car
the houses closed, the plants farmed out
goodbyes said, or not to be said
the neighbors told, the little ones in their beds

the houses closed, the plants farmed out
the station doors opening on uniform corridors
the neighbors told, the little ones in their beds
we fanned our faces, opened our books

the station doors opening on uniform corridors
then there was smoke, and damp, and sky
we fanned our faces, opened our books
we shut the windows, began to move

then there was smoke, and damp, and sky
our suitcases packed, our coats tossed off
we shut the windows, began to move
The gates were closing and the time was late

September 11

My sneakers, having taken me through a bed of poison ivy
to the window, now transfer their oils to the bath room rug
and no wonder in this time of monstrous trouble
I have knocked five times on the glass, and you have come

to open the door, for which anyone would be grateful,
your bristly head bent to the knob, round glasses reflecting
light from the glass of water that tips as you brush by,
intent on my call, so the spill sprays over the teak

in much the same way as the physics of matter
determined today that marble and steel would vaporize
or turn rubble under such pressure. Meanwhile, I'm inside
the door, returned to our hearth where the fire

place holds ivy, the summer having just closed down
and the grate in the basement covered with dust
isn't ready to be hosed down, isn't ready to open her arms
to keep us far enough, but not too far from the blaze

that we ourselves have set, unwisely,
in a house made of twigs and straw.

College Application Essay

I've gotten really good at shopping, which I'm sure
is important, because the president is always talking
about it and I'm very patriotic. I used to write little
poems and make up songs about the things I bought
but I decided that that wasn't really inside the shopping
experience, so now I try to buy things to enhance
my previous purchases, like frames for pictures,
or brooches for blouses or CDs for stereos,
and that feels right, truer. Someday I hope to become
a professional buyer. That will make all the people
who taught me shopping very proud, and I will bring
joy to all of the people I shop for. I'm a Platonic
realist, so I believe in the perfect purchase, but also
that we can never achieve it, which is both the tragedy
of life, but also what makes it worth living; the
unending pursuit of the perfect purchase, the thing
we can feel ourselves get closer and closer to,
but never actually achieve. Sometimes, I fantasize
that I've already made the perfect purchase
or that I will in the future, but it will only be revealed
to me as an epiphany in old age. I won't tell anyone,
because I will not want to brag, but it will give me
that special inner peace, that inner light of knowing
that my life did, just once, touch perfection.

Theodor Adorno

No poetry after Auschwitz. No poetry
after Armenia. No poetry after Catholic
Church, Cambodia, Tiananmen. No poetry
after slave-trade. No poetry after Wounded-
Knee, no poetry after malaria, typhoid.
No poetry after gunshot wound.
No poetry after rape. No poetry after
kaposi's sarcoma. No poetry after lupus,
ku klux klan, Shining Path.
No poetry. No poetry. No poetry.
No. No. No. No. No.

From Journal: Rai'ut Coma Ward, Tel Aviv-Yaffo, July 2003

[July 2, 2003: Reflection]

Was the air he?
Was the air she?
What tells
the beginning of this century?
On Sixth Avenue, we ate smoke
that turned the sky silver.
We plucked floating ash
from the matted wind
that got tangled in the space
where once two buildings
punctuated our stares.

[July 5, 2003: Reflection]

I was not fruitful.
I did not multiply.
Nor did I replenish.
Or fill my family's void.
I did not redeem the silenced.
No one broke through me.
From me, no one entered the world.

[July 8, 2003: Coma Ward, Prayer]

Lord, who devours us,
clarify the shape of our time here.

Tether us.
Remind us:

land is the cause,
land is the witness,

the only nation
is our breath.

On the Way to See James Dean

I hardly notice the man who gets in
at Parsons Boulevard, one seat over
from the man I swore I'd spend
the rest of my life with, read
the Sunday *Times* with, go
to the movies with to see
if James Dean is still

sexy, drinking our coffee, I say
Hon, check this out, showing him
a picture of the klan leader convicted
forty years after killing the boy
whose body was found floating
in the Tallahatchie, and the man

must have heard, without turning
his head he spits out his words:
Fuckin' faggots, fuckin'
ho-mo-sexuals. Everyone
in the subway car stops
moving, stares into their cups
or at a printed page, and I
can't tell who he's talking about
until he turns toward me, the way
psychos in movies look straight
into the camera when they say
something that makes your spine
freeze: *Fuckin' fairies*
wanna get married. Wish
I had my piece, I'd use it mother
fuckin' faggots. I look down

at my gold band, look over
at Rohan's gold band, I secretly
give up on God, Ghandi,
see myself get up, take my Uzi

from my back pocket, hand
grenade from my left shoe, my ten
queer fingers morph into switch
blades ready to cut his lips
to pieces, I open my eyes, tell
the love of my life *We should move*
to another car. But Rohan

is someone who will not be taken
down a notch or two, he tells me
he doesn't want to, so I pour
white light into the car, *Hail Mary*
full of grace, Nam-Myoho-Renge-Kyo,
Vishnu, Sebulisa, I see the people
from above, the way they say you notice
every detail in times of crisis,
your life flashes before you and you note
how the white man and the brown
had not kissed or touched, at the moment
of impact you remember every color
and nuance, you see gold
halos above the human orders seated,
you hover over the dark-skinned mom
who sits stock still, Bible
in her lap, staring at the man as if
daring him to come one inch
closer to her two pink-ribboned girls
clutching her arms in terror, you love
your neighbor, the Chinese woman
with her bag of Chinese cabbage,
the red-haired eighteen-year-old
who presses his chest into the back
of his raven-haired girlfriend, you admire
the tenacity of the Jewish man reading
from his book of prayers, each word silent
on his lips, and you love the black man
with his cane, the two girls in the corner
of the train who might be in love,

the Indian woman in her best sari,
coming home with her husband
from the mandir, which is when

you climb higher, get a wider
view of the world's delicacies, love
the diversity of ocean fish and grains
of sand, love birds of every order,
insects of every hue, the seven
miracle wonders, shore
to shore, continents smootching
other continents, you recognize how
each island, separate to the naked eye,
is connected underneath, and just
as you realize that everybody loves
the planets and the air they swim in,

you come back into the car and have
the chance to love humans of every
persuasion, even the ones who want
to bomb the hell out of every creature
still breathing. *Fuckin'*
wedding rings. I grew up in the hood
and know a faggot when I see one.
He grins at me, the way the female
soldier in the paper smiles
over the pile of naked bodies
she's standing on, ah to be pleasured
by power. There on the brink

I stand, holding pictures of people
whose heads were blown off
during morning prayer in mosques,
four girls whose bodies caught fire
in a southern church, the man
assassinated while he talked
on a porch, people living without
arms, ring fingers buried deep

in the Sunni sand. Jerusalem,
Palestine, Bali, London—on the brink
we stand, until we arrive

at West 4th Street, and we get out of the car,
checking to be sure the man doesn't follow us—
but he stays in his seat, grinning at us
through a window scratched with someone's
initials, he flips us the finger, and the train
disappears, leaving Rohan and me to argue
about the best way to walk to the theater,
we battle it out in front of perfect strangers,
salt on our popcorn, diet or regular soda,
left, right or center of the screen, and as James
Dean walks toward me, I can't make out
his terribly beautiful words.

Inner City

The young intern (we'd known her when
she was a child) – blonde, cute as a bug–
tells us how, in pediatrics, kids
come in with roaches up their noses,
in their ears. Their parents thought
they were congested, couldn't hear
so well, perhaps a cold or flu, and would
an antibiotic do the proverbial trick?
We go in with our scopes, our intern
says, *and find a leg, a fuzzy feeler,*
piece of shell. Oh, they're most often
dead . . . We're feeling creepy-
crawly now, her words inside our heads
flicking their tiny syllables, their
mandibles of sound, bearing the rigid
carapace of their dark intonations.
And what are we to do with this
bit of information, but sit here bug-eyed
in the suburbs, as outside on the new-
mown lawn, a hundred monarch butterflies
break out in the air, take wing,
and rise up in our eyes like a contagion.

The Wilders

They got their rocks off first at Highbridge Pool,
circling girls like sharks and ripping tops off.
Later came the bottoms, while the lifeguards

looked the other way and trained binoculars
on the highest dive, in case somebody
in trouble needed saving right away.

In Central Park they stripped a young woman bare
who had come to New York City to see the sights.
Her honeymoon. She hid behind her husband,

who cowered. They had knives, and teeth they showed
in grins that foretold mayhem, unrestrained,
down paths designed by Olmsted for their grace.

Soon their lives would change; they'd be recruited
like kids who came from shanties in the woods
or off the farms where they were slopping pigs.

They'd learn salute and sir and breaking in
with sticks and guns to homes where grown men huddled
and women clutched books to hidden hearts –

books they said were holy, like the prayer books
these boys carried to their First Communions.
One crossed himself before he opened fire.

In a Time of War

Flies, caught in the sap of the living
tree, some day will be
precious, dressed in amber — just so
the past appears to the present, gem-
like in its perfect preservation,
the hardened gold of yesterday, a relic
through which today's sun shines.

But those who are caught in the sticky
sap of actual time, mere insects in the odds
against them, who struggle in the ooze,
slowly sink into the mass,
the numberless, anonymous dead...
as the atrocious becomes
the mundane, our senses numb
from the sheer litany of repetition...

let us, then, just watch this one small
desperate fly, stuck first by the feet,
and then, in its struggles, entangled
entirely in the glob of sap, its wings
heavy as a brass angel's, until it is
all at once still, a dark speck
in a bubble of sap
oozing from the felled tree
in a forest marked for the mill.

How many millennia will pass
before a tear-drop lavaliere of amber
carrying its cargo of loss
will adorn the vanity of another
creature, the fly a fossil of a species
no longer present on the Earth,
the Earth itself a speck in a cosmos where
galaxies are carded like cotton on a comb

and pulled out into a distance
where some new fabric is being spun
and shimmers in the firelight
of countless, burning suns.

Afterwards

No point any more in thinking
about the big wave, a thought
you once could ride to oblivion,
a way out of a bad story, end time,
the way the Peter Weir film pulled out
the stops like hair-pins, let down
its big surprise ~ horizon gone, the sky
falling...
        white-out, the Last Wave
that ended the film, solved everything
in one final dissolve to a blank screen.

And it was all gone: conquest's white
uneasy cast, the aboriginals who saw,
drawing with sticks in the sand,
how it would come, night vision
enviable to the ones who invented light
they could switch off, hold oceans
on a strip of film, a trick of the lens,
director's cut: the sea pulls out, and out,
earth shifting its plates
as if a giant turned in his sleep~
and it all comes roaring back,
oblivion's wet wall, ground zero in motion...
but it wasn't like Weir's white-out,
only the credits coming up~
it wasn't like that at all.

*

Imagine those believers
who think "The Rapture" is for them,
who think of themselves virtually
lifted above the multitudes,
distanced from it all on the big screen
in the blue sky of a cruel delusion~
while below, the stinking beaches are littered

with bodies, and searching among them,
the desolate, like women gleaning the fields
after the harvest is done.

As if Noah, when the waters of the flood drew back,
when he saw what the waves had wrought,
could have exulted. Or the dove, with its green
meaning, returned to his trembling hand.

The Story of the Arab Who Died in the Fire

When the fire seized his body, it didn't happen by slow degrees.
No burst of heat to begin with,
no stifling billow of smoke,
no prospect of a room next door where one could escape.
The fire took him all at once,
such a thing hath not its likeness,
it peeled away his clothing,
seized upon his flesh,
the first casualties were the nerves in the skin,
then the hair was a burning fuel of fire.
God, they're burning us, he screamed,
that's all he could manage in self-defense.
The flesh was blazing along with the planks of the shed
which sustained the fire in the primary phase.
By that point his mental faculties were gone,
the firebrand of the flesh
paralyzed any sense of a future,
the memories of his family,
the links to his childhood.
He was shrieking, no longer constrained by reason,
by now all the bonds of family were broken,
he did not seek vengeance, redemption, the dawn of a new day.
All he wanted was to stop burning
but his own body kept feeding the blaze
as if he were bound and laid on the altar,
though he wasn't thinking about that, either.
He went on burning by the sheer force of his body,
flesh and fat and sinews.
And he kept on burning.
From his throat issued inhuman voices
since many human functions had already ceased
except for the pain transmitted in electrical pulses
along neural pathways to receptors in the brain.
All of that lasted no more than a single day.
And it's a good thing he gave up the ghost when he did
because he deserved to rest.

translated from the Hebrew by Chana Bloch and Chana Kronfeld

These Mountains: Selected Poems of Rivka Miriam

And You Shall Teach

And you shall teach your son muteness
that very day.
And you won't pass your caressing hand
over his features.
You'll sit your son down that very day
on the threshold of the valley
to which no man should ever come.
And you'll teach your son to sire another son.
And you'll teach him to close his eyes, to clutch
with his fist
one more night passing
and one more day.
And you shall take your son with your bare hands
that more than once embraced his mother
and with force squeeze from them your silence
which he shall give to his son.

Translated by Linda Zisquit

The Deserter

(This pacifist poem/song was written during the first Indochina War, in 1954, in the wake of WWII)

Dear Mister President
I'm writing you this letter
Perhaps you'll get to read it
If you can find the time
For I have just received
My military papers
To leave for the war
And this by Wednesday night
But Mister President
I don't want to fight
I wasn't made to kill
The wretched and the poor
I hope you won't be angry
By reading this confession
I've made a firm decision
I'm going to desert

In my short life on earth
I've seen my father die
I've seen my brothers leave
And my poor children cry
My mother knew such grief
She now lies in her grave
And mocks the bombs
And mocks the worms
When I was a POW
They took away my wife
They took away my soul
And all I know is loss
Tomorrow I'll rise early
Lock my door forever
Leave my past behind
And calmly walk away

I'll beg my way along
The gentle roads of France
From Brittany to Provence
And won't stop crying out:
Refuse to obey orders
Refuse to do it
Don't go to war
Refuse to leave
If blood must be given
Why don't you give your own
You are a good apostle
Dear Mister President
If you plan to go after me
You can warn your police
That I will not be armed
And they can safely shoot

Translated by Laure-Anne Bosselaar

Mrs. Packard

(work-in-progress, based on a true story)

"Married women and infants who, in the judgment of the medical superintendent are evidently insane or distracted, may be entered or detained in the hospital on the request of the husband of the woman or the guardian of the infant, without the evidence of insanity required in other cases."

Passed into law on February 15th, 1851, in the state of Illinois.

ILLINOIS, 1861. A theatrical space that will become many places. A grated window. Bolted doors.

SOUND OF A HEAVY PRISON DOOR CLANGS SHUT. ELIZABETH, 43, ENTERS, THROWN TO THE FLOOR BY THE IRISH MATRON, MRS. BONNER.

MRS. BONNER

Pray out loud! Ya stinkin hoor! I wanta hear ya and none of that boo-hooin' and supplicatin' to the good Lord about getting ya outta here. Yer here because yer crazy, and yer crazy, remember that! *(laughing)* That's why yer here! No more hoity-toity feelin better'n the lot of us. I'm doing no more cleanin' up after yer kind, you got that? Thinkin' yer better'n me. Ya don't think that now, do ya? Now pray, eejit—out loud!—I wanta hear ya. *(Elizabeth is silent)* Ya little witch! *(grabs her by the hair)* All yer life you sat around ordering people to do this and to do that fer ya—now it's your turn! *(she throws her down)* Pray!

ELIZABETH

Dear Lord, since I arrived in this hell on earth, King David's prayer for his persecutor has become my own... *(PAUSE)*

MRS. BONNER

(snorts)

Git on with it!

ELIZABETH

(in a whisper)

O, Lord! My persecutor remembered not to show mercy–

MRS. BONNER

Louder!

ELIZABETH

O, Lord! My persecutor remembered not to show mercy. He wanted to slay the broken in heart. Let my persecutor be clothed in shame. Let the net of mine enemy catch himself in it, and unto that same destruction let him fall. But bless thou, O Lord... And help me to forgive my husband for he knows not what he does. Amen.

MRS. BONNER brutally grabs her and hoists her up and sets her down hard in a chair.

MRS. BONNER

Wait here.

MRS. BONNER EXITS. ELIZABETH SITS IN A CHAIR for a few moments alone. She tries to straighten her hair, her dress. THEOPHILUS, her husband, 57, AND DR. MCFARLAND, a good-looking 44, ENTER.

DR. MCFARLAND

Mrs. Packard, how do you do. I am Dr. McFarland, the Superintendent of Jacksonville Insane Asylum. Welcome. Reverend Packard, take a seat. I would like to have a discussion with you, Mrs. Packard, with your husband present before he leaves you here with us. You will in future be in my personal care.

ELIZABETH

(charming, almost flirtatious)

How do you do, Doctor? I am so glad to hear it—that you will be in charge of my personal care. *(laughs)* I don't know why it is, Doctor, it may be merely a foolish pride, but I can't help feeling an instinctive aversion to being called insane. There seems to be a kind of disparagement of intellect attending this idea, which seems to stain the purity and darken the luster of the reputation forever after. Don't you agree?

DR. MCFARLAND

(equally charmed)

No, no, Mrs. Packard, this is not necessarily so. Even some of the most renowned and gifted minds in the world have been insane, and their reputation and character are still revered and respected—some of our greatest poets even—

ELIZABETH

Indeed. Yes... How true—

DR. MCFARLAND

Your husband tells me that your father thought it right to educate you as well as his sons! So you, my good woman, have a great love of reading and intellectual discourse. Is that right?

ELIZABETH

Yes. Quite right.

DR. MCFARLAND

Well, I intend for you to enjoy special privileges while you are here, Mrs. Packard, and will be sure to furnish you with books of your choosing and perhaps you and I will be able to converse together as well. I should like that.

ELIZABETH

Why, thank you, Doctor. How kind of you. Though my Bible will be my most cherished book.

DR. MCFARLAND

Of course. I did not mean to suggest otherwise. Now... *(looking in his file)*
I do hope you slept well and that the plain food of the asylum will agree with you.

ELIZABETH

Quite frankly, doctor, though my room is quite clean, my bed is narrow and hard and I am unused to sleeping alone.

(Theophilus shifts uncomfortably. The doctor smiles, charmed.)

DR. MCFARLAND

Really? I understand.

ELIZABETH

When I ceased, only recently, to have the warmth of my once dear husband in bed beside me, I brought the youngest of my children into bed with me so that I could sleep. This my husband well knows. So, no, I did not sleep well, I thank you. I could not.

DR. MCFARLAND

I hope that will improve as you get used to your new surroundings. Mrs. Packard, how many children did you say you have?

ELIZABETH

I did not say. At the time of my kidnapping, my husband and I had been married 21 years. We have 6 children, five boys and a girl. The oldest is 18 years old and the youngest 18 months. All except the oldest were living at home the morning I was abducted.

DR. MCFARLAND

Abducted? Isn't that a rather strong word?

ELIZABETH

Not in the least. I was abducted, or kidnapped, whichever word you prefer. Yesterday, while I was having my bath, I saw out the window two strong- men, a sheriff, two doctors, and my husband come into the house. They proceeded to climb up the stairs to my bedroom door. Theophilus shouted they were coming in. Alarmed, I got up and locked the door. I said: please wait. He said: they would not wait, they were taking me away to the asylum, and that I better unlock the door or they would break it down. They proceeded to hack down the door with an axe. I raced, completely naked, under the covers, terrified. The men stormed in. My pulse was racing, as any proper woman's pulse would under the circumstances. The doctor took my hand, felt my pulse, said "Her pulse is very quick" and pronounced me insane. The second doctor did the same. When I said to my husband 'you can't do this! I am perfectly sane, and you know it!' he just laughed and told me to get dressed at once. When I refused to walk downstairs to the waiting wagon, the two strong men carried me onto the wagon and when we arrived at the station, they carried me off the wagon onto the waiting train. *(pause)* I was abducted. Don't you agree?

DOCTOR MCFARLAND

(nods)

I see you did not come on your own volition.

ELIZABETH

I take it I am here because I disagree with my husband's theological views, and I voiced those disagreements in Bible class?

DR. MCFARLAND

Your husband is concerned about your sanity, Mrs. Packard, and wants you to have professional care.

ELIZABETH

My only offence as far as I can tell in 21 years of marriage is that I have dared to be true to my honest convictions and to give utterance to these views in my husband's church. Husband, Christ's cause is not so weak that it needs your protection.

DR. MCFARLAND

Mrs. Packard, come, come. We are not here to discuss why your husband brought you here. As you now know, he has every right to do so.

ELIZABETH

Doctor, my husband is jealous of my ability to reach people because he cannot. His congregation is dwindling. He preaches a hard sermon and a cold religion. There were four men in the Bible class before I went and encouraged healthy discussion. There were 42 men and women when I was told to stop six weeks later! And it would have grown larger. Our classes became a place of animating discussion. For the first time, we freely and openly discussed Calvinist doctrine. As a good Christian woman, I cannot believe in the strict Calvinist view of original sin. This is not insanity. The Jesus I worship and love does not blame women for all that is evil in the world! And I am not alone in thinking that!

THEOPHILUS

(finally speaking)

You see, Doctor? There is no controlling her. She flies into these fits frequently. This is what I have been living with and what I hope you will cure.

DOCTOR MCFARLAND

Did you ever publicly defy your husband, Mrs. Packard?

LONG PAUSE.

THEOPHILUS

She did.

ELIZABETH

I did.

DOCTOR MCFARLAND

Go on.

ELIZABETH

Once when Mr. Packard was at the pulpit I asked for the congregation and the minister's blessing to leave the church and worship with the Methodists where my personal beliefs could be respected.

THEOPHILUS

She exposed her irrationality and perversity to full public view. The entire congregation saw she had gone mad.

DOCTOR MCFARLAND

How long would you say your disagreements have been a problem between you and your husband, Mrs. Packard?

ELIZABETH

The last year or so, I should think.

THEOPHILUS shakes his head.

DOCTOR MCFARLAND

Reverend Packard?

THEOPHILUS

The last ten years. At least.

Elizabeth looks at him, aghast.

Her mother was mad as well, Doctor, you should know, and Mrs. Packard herself was committed to an asylum once before, when she was young.

ELIZABETH

I was put in hospital for brain fever—delirium and fever—not madness, as my husband well knows. And my mother was not mad, Doctor. That is completely false. She did weep often but that was understandable. She had lost five children under the age of three, and she did grieve for them.

THEOPHILUS

It is a simple case of moral perversity.

DOCTOR MCFARLAND

Yes, most insanity starts as such. However, though moral perversity is an institutionable disorder, in most cases it can be cured, if the patient is willing. Mr. Packard, I leave you with your wife to say good-bye... (he rises) Mrs. Packard, let me remind you that you will have every special privilege here while under my watch. Quite frankly, I shouldn't think you will be here very long. Good day to you both.

HE takes her hand. SHE holds it for a moment looking deeply into his eyes.

ELIZABETH

Doctor.

DOCTOR MCFARLAND

It has been a... very great pleasure to meet you, Mrs. Packard.

He then shakes Theo's hand as HE exits, leaving Theo with Elizabeth. There is a long, long silence. Neither speaks. Finally, with great control:

ELIZABETH

You see, husband, the doctor does not think me mad.

THEOPHILUS

You are wrong there, Mrs. Packard. Believe me.

ELIZABETH

I am not mad, husband, and well you know it!...do you know where you are leaving me? This is an awful, awful place. It is a prison, Theo, I am begging you. The matron threw me on the floor this morning. Theo, please. I shall die here.

THEOPHILUS

I am sorry to hear you talk so. I had hoped we should have at least a pleasant parting.

ELIZABETH looks at him, aghast.

You will thank me in years to come, I am sure. You will see I, too, had no recourse. In answer to your question of your having the right to think your own thoughts, my answer to you is this, as I have told you repeatedly. You may think your own thoughts when you are thinking right. And once you are thinking right, you may return home. You endanger the souls of your family and yourself as you are now. I sincerely hope you will be cured, Elizabeth. Good-day.

HE thinks of embracing her and then can not. HE exits. ELIZABETH throws herself against the wall, sobbing.....

DR. MCFARLAND enters.

DR. MCFARLAND

Well, Mrs. Packard. Your husband has just left us for the train station. I have never seen a man so deeply afflicted and even heartbroken as Mr. Packard was at parting with you. He broke into tears when he saw me. If ever a man manifested true and deep affection for his wife—

ELIZABETH

Doctor! I have never seen a face more radiant with joy than my husband's just now when he waved good-bye to me from the street. He could only be described as triumphant, having incarcerated his unruly wife with no opposition. *(she glares at him)*

DOCTOR MCFARLAND

I see. We will not discuss it now...You have been admitted to Ward number 7. It is the best ward in the hospital. You will be having your breakfast meal soon. Meals are taken with all the inmates, though your table of women will all be from the seventh ward. Mrs. Bonner will explain the rules to you. Good morning.

Contributors

Kim Addonizio's most recent poetry collection is *What Is This Thing Called Love* (W.W. Norton). She is also the author of a novel, *Little Beauties* (Simon & Schuster). She lives in Oakland, CA.

Anita Barrows has written four books of poetry and has translated poetry, plays, fiction and non-fiction from French, German, and Italian. Most recently she has translated (with Joanna Macy) selections from Rilke's *Sonnets to Orpheus* and *Duino Elegies* (Riverhead, 2005). She lives in Berkeley where she is a clinical psychologist and a grandmother.

Robin Becker's sixth collection of poems, *Domain of Perfect Affection* (2006), has just come out with the University of Pittsburgh Press which also published three previous collections: *The Horse Fair* (2000); *All-American Girl* (1996 Lambda Award for Lesbian Poetry); and *Giacometti's Dog* (1990). Becker's awards include individual fellowships from the Bunting Institute, the Massachusetts Cultural Council, and the National Endowment for the Arts. Becker's poetry column, "Field Notes," is a regular feature of *The Women's Review of Books* where she serves as Contributing and Poetry Editor.

Dan Bellm, San Francisco poet and translator, is the author of two collections, *One Hand on the Wheel* (Heyday Books) and *Buried Treasure* (Cleveland State University). His poems have also appeared in *The Best American Spiritual Writing, Poetry, Tikkun, Ploughshares, The Threepenny Review* and other journals and anthologies.

Laure-Anne Bosselaar is the author of *The Hour Between Dog and Wolf* and *of Small Gods of Grief*, winner of the Isabella Gardner Prize in 2001. In 2005, Four Way Books published her fourth anthology, *Never Before: Poems About First Experiences.*

Kurt Brown is the author of four full-length books of poetry, and five award-winning chapbooks. He is the editor of many poetry anthologies, including *Drive, They Said: Poems about Americans and their Cars* and *Verse & Universe: Poems about Science and Mathematics.* He lives in New York City, and teaches at Sarah Lawrence College in Bronxville, New York.

Chris Bursk is the author of nine books, most recently *The Improbable Swervings of Atoms* from the University of Pittsburgh Press and *The First Inhabitants of Arcadia* from the University of Arkansas Press. Recipient of PEW, NEW, and Guggenheim

Fellowships, for a number of years he volunteered in the Bucks County Correctional system and worked for Bucks County Community College.

Hayden Carruth has published fifty books, chiefly poems, but including one novel, two anthologies, a book about jazz, and several collections of essays and reviews. From 1979 to 1991 he taught in the graduate writing program at Syracuse University. He and his wife, the poet Joe-Anne McLaughlin, live in upstate New York.

Jan Clausen, a NYFA poetry fellow for 2003, has published in *Bloom, Fence, North American Review, Ploughshares,* and elsewhere. Her most recent book is a memoir, *Apples and Oranges.*

Chard deNiord is the author of three books of poetry, *Night Mowing* (The University of Pittsburgh Press, 2005). *Sharp Golden Thorn* (Marsh Hawk Press, 2003), and *Asleep in the Fire* (University of Alabama Press, 1990). He is an associate professor of English at Providence College and directs the low residency MFA program in poetry at New England College. He lives in Putney, Vermont.

Martin Desht first began documenting post-industrial cities and towns in Pennsylvania, once the most heavily and diversely industrialized state in the nation, in 1989. "Faces from an American Dream" not only records a vanishing industrial landscape, it explores how this rapid social change had re-defined the American industrial city and had altered the personal attainment of the American dream for skilled and unskilled workers by the end of the twentieth century. Desht is a graduate of DeSales University and of the Master of Fine Arts Poetry Program at New England College. He is currently finishing a manuscript that combines his urban poems with his photographs for a book to accompany the exhibit.

Denise Duhamel's most recent poetry titles are *Two and Two* (University of Pittsburgh Press, 2005), *Mille et un Sentiments* (Firewheel, 2005), and *Queen for a Day: Selected and New Poems* (Pittsburgh, 2001). She teaches poetry at Florida International University in Miami.

Stephen Dunn is the author of fourteen collections of poetry, the most recent of which is *Everything Else in the World.* His *Different Hours* won the 2001 Pulitzer Prize. He lives in Frostburg, Maryland.

Ann Fisher-Wirth is the author of two books of poems (*Blue Window* and *Five Terraces*) and two chapbooks (*The Trinket Poems* and *Walking Wu Wei's Scroll*). Her awards include a Malahat Review Long Poem Prize, the Rita Dove Poetry Award, the Poetry Award from the Mississippi Institute of Arts and Letters, and two Poetry Fellowships from the Mississippi Arts Commission. Her poems have appeared widely in journals, online, and in anthologies. She teaches at the University of Mississippi.

Jeff Friedman's fourth collection of poems, *Black Threads*, will be published by Carnegie Mellon University Press in fall 2006.

Ross Gay's book, *Against Which*, is published by CavanKerry Press. He is a Cave Canem fellow, a former Bread Loaf scholar, and a basketball coach. He teaches poetry at Montclair St. University and in New England College's low-residency MFA program.

Reginald Gibbons' most recent books of poems are *It's Time* (LSU, 2002) and two chapbooks, *In the Warhouse* (Fractal Edge, 2004) and *Fern-Texts* (Hollyridge, 2005). He also published a translation of *Antigone*, with co-translator Charles Segal, in 2003 (Oxford).

Albert Goldbarth has twice been the recipient of the National Book Critics Circle Award in poetry, and has also published four collections of essays and a novel. His newest collection, *Budget Travel Through Space and Time* was released by Graywolf Press.

Jim Haba, Director of the Geraldine R. Dodge Poetry Program, designs and produces the biennial Dodge Poetry Festival and also oversees the Program's various poetry activities for New Jersey high school students and teachers at every grade level. A painter as well as a poet, he lives in central New Jersey.

Marilyn Hacker is the author of eleven books of poems, most recently *Desesperanto*, published by W.W. Norton in 2003, along with *First Cities: Collected Early Poems.* She received the Lenore Marshall Award of the Academy of American poets in 1995 for *Winter Numbers*, which also received a Lambda Literary Award; her *Selected Poems* received the Poets' Prize in 1996. She received the Prix Max Jacob Etranger in France in 2005 for *La Rue palimpseste* (translated into French by Claire Malroux) She has published four recent books of translations: *A Long-Gone Sun* (Sheep Meadow Press, 2000) and *Birds and Bison* (Sheep Meadow Press, 2005) both of poems by Claire Malroux, and *Here There Was Once a Country* (Oberlin College Press, 2001) and *She Says* (Graywolf Press, 2003) both by Vénus Khoury-Ghata. Hacker received an Award in Literature from the American Academy of Arts and Letters in 2004. She lives in New York and Paris, and teaches at the City College of New York and the CUNY Graduate Center.

Donald Hall's "Gospel" is from *White Apples and the Taste of Stone: New and Selected Poems*. His previous book was *The Best Day the Worst Day*, a prose memoir of his marriage to Jane Kenyon and her death.

Eloise Klein Healy, Founding Chair of the MFA in Creative Writing Program at Antioch University Los Angeles and Distinguished Professor Emerita, is a Guest Poet at the Idyllwild Summer Poetry Festival. Healy is co-founder of ECO-ARTS, an eco-tourism/arts venture, and founding editor of *ARKTOI*, an imprint of Red Hen Press.

Lorraine Healy is an Argentinean poet and photographer living on Whidbey Island, Washington. The author of two published chapbooks, she received a Pushcart Prize nomination in 2004. She is a recent graduate from the M.F.A program at New England College, New Hampshire.

Jane Hirshfield's sixth collection of poetry, *AFTER*, was published by HarperCollins in February 2006. Recipient of the Academy of American Poets 70th Annual Fellowship for Distinguished Writing as well as a recent NEA fellowship, her poems and essays also appear in *The American Poetry Review, Ploughshares, Threepenny Review, Orion,* and *New Letters.*

Ilya Kaminsky's *Dancing In Odessa* won the Whiting Writers Award, American Academy of Arts and Letters' Metcalf Award and was *ForeWord Magazine*'s Best Book of 2005.

Marilyn Krysl's poems have appeared in *The Atlantic, The Nation, The New Republic, the Pushcart Prize Anthology*, and stories in *Best American Short Stories 2000, O. Henry Prize Stories.* Her latest books are *Warscape With Lovers* (Cleveland State Poetry Center), and *How To Accommodate Men* (Coffee House). She served as Artist in Residence at the Center for Human Caring, worked as a volunteer for Peace Brigade International in Sri Lanka, and volunteered at the Kalighat Home for the Destitute and Dying administered by Mother Teresa's Sisters of Charity in Calcutta. In Boulder she volunteers with the Lost Boys of Sudan and C-SAW, the Community of Sudanese and American Women.

Joan Larkin has published four collections of poetry, including *Cold River*. Her recent writing includes *Brother Dust*, a hip-hop version of Sophocles' *Antigone*.

Dorianne Laux's fourth book of poems, *Facts about the Moon*, has been recently published by W.W. Norton.

David Lehman's recent books of poetry include *When a Woman Loves a Man* (Scribner, 2005) and *The Evening Sun* (2002).

Anne Marie Macari's second book, *Gloryland*, was published in 2005 by Alice James Books. Her first book, *Ivory Cradle*, won the APR/Honickman first book prize in 2000. Her poems have appeared in numerous magazines such as *The Iowa Review, The American Poetry Review* and *Five Points*. Macari teaches at the New England College low-residency MFA program.

Emily Mann is celebrating her 17th season at McCarter Theatre, where directing credits include the world premieres of *Miss Witherspoon* (also Off-Broadway), *The Bells and Last of the Boys*; Nilo Cruz's Pulitzer Prize-winning *Anna in the Tropics* (also on Broadway), *Uncle Vanya* (also adapted), *All Over* (also off-Broadway, 2003 Obie Award for her direction), *Romeo and Juliet, The Cherry Orchard* (also adapted), Meshugah (author/adaptor), *The Mai, Twilight: Los Angeles, 1992, The Perfectionist, Miss Julie* (also adapted), *Three Sisters, Betsey Brown* (co-author), *The Glass Menagerie*, and most recently, *The Birthday Party*. Her plays include the award-winning *Execution of Justice, Still Life* (six Obie Awards), *Greensboro* (A Requiem), and *Annulla, An Autobiography*. Ms. Mann wrote and directed *Having Our Say*, adapted from the book by Sarah L. Delany and A. Elizabeth Delany with Amy Hill Hearth (3 Tony nominations including Best Play and Best Direction, and a Peabody Award for the screenplay). A winner of the Dramatists' Guild Hull-Warriner Award, she is a member of the Dramatists Guild and serves on its Council. In 2002 she received an Honorary Doctorate of Arts from Princeton University.

Pablo Medina was born in Havana, Cuba. He is the author of ten books of poetry and prose, most recently *The Cigar Roller: A Novel* (Grove, 2005) and *Points of Balance/Puntos de apoyo*, a bilingual collection of poems (Four Way, 2005). He is on the faculties of Eugene Lang College, The New School for the Liberal Arts, and the Warren Wilson MFA Program for Writers. On March 2005 he was elected to a one-year term as president of AWP (The Association of Writers and Writing Programs.

D.H. Melhem poet: seventh collection, *New York Poems* (Syracuse Univ. Press, 2005); novelist: *Blight* (distributed by SUP); scholar: *Gwendolyn Brooks*; *Heroism in the New Black Poetry*; editor: two anthologies; musical drama, *Children of the House Afire*, produced at Theater for the New City; over 60 essays. Honors include NEH fellowship and American Book Award. Forthcoming 2007: *Stigma* and *The Cave* (SUP), final two novels of trilogy *Patrimonies*.

Rivka Miriam was born in Jerusalem in 1952; she continues to live and work there. Her father was the Yiddish writer Leib Rochman. Her first poetry collection was published in 1966, when she was 14. She has published eleven books of poetry, two collections of short stories and two children's books. Her books include *Poems of Stone Mothers* (1988), *Place, Tiger* (1994) *Nearby Was the East* (1996), *Resting Jew* (2000) and *Said the Investigator* (2005). She has received numerous literary awards, and has twice been awarded the Prime Minister's Award. She is also a painter who has exhibited in solo and group shows. She is head of Elul, an important Jerusalem Jewish Studies center

Ed Ochester's most recent book is *The Land Of Cockaigne* (Story Line Press, 2001). Forthcoming is *Unreconstructed: Poems Selected And New* (Autumn House, 2007) and *The Living Poem* (University of Pittsburgh Press, 2007), an anthology of contemporary American poetry. He edits the Pitt Poetry Series and is general editor of the Drue Heinz Literature Prize for short fiction (both University of Pittsburgh Press). From 1978 to 1998 he was director of the writing program at the University of Pittsburgh, and was twice elected president of Associated Writing Programs. He co-edits the poetry magazine *5 AM* and is a core faculty member of the Bennington College MFA program.

Alicia Ostriker is twice a finalist for the National Book Award. Her most recent book of poems is *No Heaven*, published by the University of Pittsburgh Press. Ostriker is Professor of English at Rutgers University and teaches in the New England College low-residency MFA Program in poetry.

Robert Pinsky's most recent books are *Jersey Rain* (poems) and *The Life of David* (prose).

Hilda Raz is the Luschei Endowed Editor of *Prairie Schooner* and the founding editor of the Prairie Schooner Prize Book Series in Fiction and Poetry. A book of essays written with Aaron Raz Link, *What Becomes You*, is forthcoming. *Divine Honors* and *Trans* were published by Wesleyan UP.

Dahlia Ravikovitch (1936-2005), one of Israel's great poets - perhaps the greatest Hebrew woman poet of all time - was widely known for her outspoken and courageous political activism.

Jason Schneiderman is the author of *Sublimation Point* from Four Way Books. His work has appeared in *Tin House, The Best American Poetry 2005, Ninth Letter, Spork, The Penguin Book of the Sonnet*, and elsewhere. A recipient of fellowships from Yaddo, and the Fine Arts Work Center in Provincetown, he is currently a Chancellor's Fellow at the Graduate Center of the City University of New York.

Yerra Sugarman's first book, *Forms of Gone*, was published by The Sheep Meadow Press in 2002, and received the 2005 PEN/Joyce Osterweil Award for Poetry and a "Discovery"/The Nation Prize, among others. Her poems have been appeared in many journals, and have been translated into French. She teaches at NYU and City College.

Richard Tayson's second book of poetry, *The World Underneath,* is forthcoming from the Kent State University Press in 2007. His first book of poetry, *The Apprentice of Fever,* won the Wick Poetry Prize. Recent prose appears in *Virginia Quarterly Review, The Gay and Lesbian Review* and *Pleiades.* Tayson is a Chancellor's Fellow at the Graduate Center, City University of New York.

Ronald Wallace is the author of twelve books of poetry, fiction, and criticism, the most recent being *Long For This World: New And Selected Poems* (University of Pittsburgh Press). He co-directs the creative writing program at the University of Wisconsin-Madison, and serves as poetry editor for the University of Wisconsin Press. He divides his time between Madison and a 40-acre farm in Bear Valley, Wisconsin.

Irene Willis is the author of two books of poems, *They Tell Me You Danced* (University Press of Florida, 1995), and *At the Fortune Café*, winner of the Violet Reed Haas Prize for Poetry, Snake Nation Press, 2005.

Eleanor Wilner's most recent book is *The Girl With Bees in her Hair* (Copper Canyon, 2004). She teaches in the MFA Program for Writers, Warren Wilson College.

Boris Vian was born at Ville d'Avray, France, in 1920. Trained as a civil engineer, he was also a poet, jazz trumpeter, novelist, screen-writer, film actor, cabaret singer, translator, and inventor. Vian was an active part of a leftist movement who protested against the Algerian war, and his song *Le Déserteur* was banned by the French government. He died in Paris in 1959.

SENECA REVIEW

Vol. XXXVI, No. 1

Eugénio de Andrade
Edward Bartók-Baratta
Marianne Boruch
Carol Burbank
Teresa Cader
Gerald Chapple
Mary Crow
John Crutchfield
D.W. Cunningham
Jim Daniels
Christopher Dombrowski
Lauren Fanelli
Susan Goslee
Eamon Grennan
Megan Grumbling
Daniel Gutstein
Ed Haworth Hoeppner
Roberto Juarroz
Günter Kunert
Melissa Kwasny
Alexis Levitin
Susan Lewis
Terri McCord
Kevin McFadden
Andrew Mister
Melissa Morphew
Muriel Nelson
Amy Newman
Martha Ronk
Natania Rosenfeld
Sandra Simonds
Paul West
Nancy White
Grace Wilentz
Roger Williams
Jason Zuzga

New Poems and Lyric Essays

Translations from the German, Portuguese, and Spanish

Please send me _____copy(ies) of Vol. XXXVI, No. 1 at $7 each.
Please enter my subscription for _____year(s) beginning with issue_____.
Rates: $11/year; $20/2 years. *Seneca Review* is published twice yearly, spring and fall.
Make check payable to *Seneca Review* and mail orders to Deborah Tall, Editor, *Seneca Review*, Hobart and William Smith Colleges, Geneva, NY 14456. Or visit our website at: www.hws.edu/SenecaReview

Name____

Address______________________________________

____

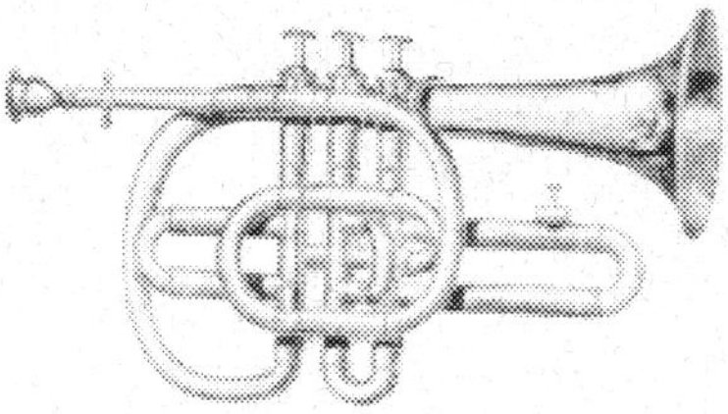

The Mississippi Review
www.mississippireview.com

art
against
bananas

The Center for Writers
The University of Southern Mississippi
118 College Drive # 5144
Hattiesburg, MS 39406-5144

WANT TO READ ABOUT POETRY?

REVIEW REVUE

WHERE CONTEMPORARY POETRY
INTERSECTS WITH CRITICISM

A JOURNAL OF REVIEWS, INTERVIEWS AND
PROSODY ESSAYS

If you haven't read *Review Revue*, here's what you've missed so far: conversations with Lucille Clifton and David St. John; Stephen Dunn on Poetry in a Consumer Society, Annie Finch on the Body of Poetry, and Kurt Brown on Postmodernism: The Reluctant Revolution; a forum of university press editors talking about their work; Denise Lowe on gender and poetry; and reviews of Adrienne Rich, Peter Johnson, Steve Orlen, Jean Valentine, Russell Edson, Jack Gilbert, and Brigit Pegeen Kelly; and regular reviews of Contemporary Classics. Join the conversation *about* poetry!

Try it! It's tri-annual!

Current issue: $5.00 (ppd) A 3-issue subscription: $10.00 (ppd)

Review Revue | PO Box 13061 | Lansing, MI 48901

For information about reviews, ads, classroom subscriptions, and other information visit our website:
home.earthlink.net/~glafemina/reviewrevue

Back Issues From 1980s and 1990s Available
Call: (301) 687-4024 or E-mail: nightsun@frostburg.edu

Back
Issues
Available!
nightsun@frostburg.edu

Nightsun

Issue 23 Guest-Edited By: STEPHEN DUNN
Issue 24 Guest-Edited By: ROBLEY WILSON